To Become A Racehorse Trainer

To Become A Racehorse Trainer

Joe Hartigan

J. A. Allen
London

ISBN 0 85131 234 9

Published in 1975 by J.A. Allen & Company Limited,
1 Lower Grosvenor Place, Buckingham Palace Road,
London, SW1W 0EL.

Design by Bill Ireson

Printed and bound by The Devonshire Press Ltd.,
Torquay.

Contents

Contents

Foreword

I first met Joe Hartigan nearly thirty years ago on the day he successfully partnered General McCreery's Jumbo at an Army meeting in Vienna soon after the end of the war. In the years between I have met him at odd times on the racecourse and I was therefore delighted when he asked me to write a Foreword to this book which I have so much enjoyed reading.

Joe Hartigan has spent his whole life in racing and was, as it were, reared on the milk of it. I feel sure that any young man setting out to try his luck as a trainer will find this book full of interest and useful information which will be of tremendous help to him.

Training racehorses is very largely a matter of using one's commonsense and remembering that horses are not machines. Treat them as individuals and be with them as much as possible. In this way one quickly learns their characters. Be content to make slow progress and, especially when teaching young animals their business, never try to do too much in one day. If a racehorse receives a gradual preparation he will do his work happily and because he enjoys it will in nearly every case give of his best.

A trainer's life is never a dull one and although there are plenty of ups and downs the excitement and thrill of seeing one of yours "go by the stick" makes up for the disappointments that are bound to come your way. There is always something to look forward to and as a way of life it takes all the beating in the world.

In the following pages Joe Hartigan has given the reader the real feeling of his life as a trainer.

Introduction

" 'Tis only a trainer who knows a trainer's cares." This old maxim is one I heard as soon as I was old enough to take in anything, and although it may well be a misquote, referring to some profession other than that of a racehorse trainer, it certainly meets the case.

If your heart is set on becoming a racehorse trainer, you will learn the wisdom of those words. But my object is not to put off people; rather it is to encourage those who are prepared to take up the challenge, and if possible to help them avoid some of the pitfalls into which I blundered during my 18 years as a trainer.

I

Starting the Job

To start any job as a self-employed person is something of a gamble, but in the case of taking out a licence to train racehorses it is a larger one, in my opinion. A lot depends on how much capital one has, and how many rich friends one has to become owners. The less one has of either, the gloomier the picture becomes.

When I took the plunge, I remember the advice of the only two people I asked. Noel Murless and Willie Stephenson both gave me encouragement in their own way.

In 1952 my father died, and as he had made his will in the good old-fashioned style (in 1936) I found that what cash was left after his 50 years of training went to my children. As I did not marry until 1958, this was no help at the time!

However, by a bit of wangling the sum of £3,000 emerged from the wreck to start me off. I had seen enough of the job to realise that it was no longer a paying concern and when I put my doubts to Noel, to whom I was assistant trainer, and who in turn had learned the job with my father and uncle, he said: "If I had thought about the money side like you are doing, I would never have started, let alone got to the position I am today." When I asked Willie Stephenson if he thought there was still any hope of making it pay, he said: "Of course not! But in what other job would you be able to live so well and get so much fun?"

I have quoted my own start as a trainer merely to illustrate how we all felt about the job 21 years ago, and not because I have any intention of making an autobiography out of this book. From now on I will try to explain the various problems which the would-be trainer will have to face.

To take over a stable of high-class horses is a trainer's dream, and there is a lot of truth in the saying that "good horses make good trainers and jockeys". You cannot go far wrong if you step into someone else's shoes, either as a private trainer or public one. You must, of course, have knowledge and experience; but given these you should do as well as your predecessor, provided the high-class horses prove as good as they look on paper.

Another fairly sure way to success as a trainer is to be a rich man in your own right. In this way you can have a very enjoyable life owning your own horses when necessary and training for yourself, if you find you can't stick the owners. You can always go out and buy a better horse when you find the existing set-up is no good and so put yourself back on the map.

However, neither the rich man, nor the fortunate one who has been handed over a good stable, comes into this book, which is aimed at the brave man who starts up as a trainer with all the necessary knowledge but very little else. In this case it is a matter of renting a yard, not buying one. There is the question of tack to be taken care of. A car is a necessity and if the money runs to it, a horse-box is a good investment.

It has often been said by trainers that the best paying concern in the yard is the horse-box, and although these days the Road Fund Tax and insurance keeps increasing, the drivers' hours are governed, and the cost of the vehicle is frightening, it should still pay its way. The ideal situation for a trainer running his own horse-box is to train about 25 to 30 horses and hold a licence for both Flat and jumping. He should employ a driver who is also travelling head-lad and a good stableman capable of riding work, or if need be, drive the box himself. In this way, provided one has no major troubles with the horse-box and can keep it on the road as often as possible, at least £500 per year should be made, without charging owners as much as public transport would have to charge. It is, in fact, the best horse in the yard, but a large stable will find that it has to hire most of the time in any case, because the three or four-stall horse-box is not sufficient to deal with all the runners, and a small stable of say 12 to 15 horses will not find enough work for the box. It is also uneconomical to employ a man just to drive the box; he must fulfil another useful role at home — even if by modern restrictions he is not supposed to do anything apart from sleep whilst at the racecourse!

The question of tack is quite an item for the new trainer and perhaps the best way to deal with it is to attend an auction of a trainer who has either died or gone broke. Second-hand saddles, bridles, head-collars etc. are on the whole good value. The leather of 30 years ago seems to outlast the modern stuff (although you will not find a saddler to agree with this view!). You can see for yourself how long it takes before a *new* girth or surcingle strap has all its holes run together; whereas if you stitch on an old strap (even 50 years old) it will last a lifetime. Provided the saddles have sound trees and are ordinary 10lb exercise saddles, and the bridles, head collars, rugs, exercise sheets etc. are in fair nick — buy them all at a sale. The only items of tack which it is necessary to buy new are paddock sheets with your initials boldly displayed, to show the racing world that you mean business.

The renting of a yard is, of course, the first move, and by far the most important one.

In England many of the racing stables and gallops which come up for sale or lease have been changing hands for the last 150 years. Unfortunately, these yards are nearly all in existing racing areas.

I always wanted to be on my own and not, as the force of circumstances dictated, cheek by jowl with other trainers. However, it is highly probable that a new trainer will find, as I did, that he is forced to rent a stable in Newmarket, Epsom, Lambourn, Middleham or Malton.

In this case there are definite advantages. Adequate gallops are laid on at a charge of so much per horse, which you can pass straight on to your patrons. Owners feel they are more "in the swim" if they can tell their friends that their horses are trained at one of these centres. Labour, although more apt to swap stables, is more abundant. Jockeys are usually on the spot to ride work for you. Transport for yourself and your horses can become a joint enterprise with your neighbours.

The disadvantages are, I must confess, fewer, and my only grumbles were that since a horse likes different ground to work on, the sheer monotony of using the same bit of turf, as laid down by the authority which runs the gallops, becomes a bore to both the horse and yourself. In deference to your neighbour you find yourself either paying more wages to your lads to keep abreast or charging less to your owner in order to stop your neighbour from pinching him too!

If you are lucky enough to have your own private training place, at least 10 miles away from anyone else, you can look after your own gallops and spend hours working out how to improve them, which is a great interest besides being an essential. Your staff will be entirely your own concern. If they like you, they will work for you; if you lose them, you know it is your fault. Finally, you will avoid a lot of petty quarrels with your trainer neighbours which can happen over the swapping of staff and owners in a closely-knit racing area.

There is a certain amount of superstition in all branches of racing, as no doubt there is in any business which relies to a large extent on luck. A stable which has a name for being unlucky is perhaps best left alone. It might not be just bad luck which has caused the previous tenants to quit after a few years with a lack of winners. It could be to do with the stables themselves, the gallops, even the water which the horses drink, or perhaps the altitude does not suit.

When one looks at what appears to be an ideal training establishment, yet it has produced remarkably few winners, I think one should not rush in with the attitude of — "Those other chaps could not train ivy up a wall and I will soon produce the goods". However good you are, or think you are, you should consider the fact that some of the previous occupants may have been equally talented, yet they had failed.

Another important factor when choosing a stable is the lads' accommodation. In the same way that a cavalry man was taught at the end of the day that his horse was the first priority, a trainer in these times has to put his lads first and himself last. If the house that you are about to live in leaves something to be desired, don't worry unduly, provided you have a good set-up to cater for your staff. I am not saying this with my tongue in my cheek. The trainer can always move to a nearby house, but his head man and apprentices must have proper accommodation if that trainer is to keep a contented staff on the place.

It is essential that you have either yourself or the head man on the spot, and of the two the head man is the most important. You will obviously be away at times, possibly as often as three nights a week, and it is for the head man to see that your horses are all right and that the apprentices don't set fire to the barn!

The number of loose boxes depends so much on the rent

15

which you can afford. But to make a living you really need at least 30 horses and a paddock or two for turning out horses and to exercise in during bad weather. Nowadays I suppose it will mean a minimum of £1,000 a year rent, but a larger place will be considerably more; and when one considers the rates, electricity, heating etc., it seems wiser to look for the 30-horse yard, and hope to fill every box with a fully paid-for tenant. If you hit the jackpot, you can build more boxes with the landlord's consent.

2

Collecting Owners

Once the important job of selecting the right yard is settled, it is time to produce the required number of horses to obtain a licence.

I think that you need at least seven young horses, and that perhaps four two-year-olds and three three-year-olds would just get you a licence for the Flat. However, unlike obtaining a dog licence or T.V. licence, the trainer's application is given careful thought by the Jockey Club before a licence is granted. This is as it should be, and it is why I hesitate about the number of seven horses being sufficient. It depends a lot on who you are and what qualifications you hold, and also on the suitability of the yard and gallops which you have acquired.

When racing is faced with a situation whereby there are far more horses in training than can be comfortably dealt with, the authorities are becoming rather choosy about granting trainers' licences. This is no doubt why people with such good qualifications as Fred Winter were turned down when applying for a Flat race licence. In view of this, I would advise a young man starting up as a trainer to inquire first before he signs the lease on his new establishment.

Messrs Weatherby are by no means unapproachable and it will be as well to tackle them as follows — "I have recently arranged to rent such-and-such a yard and intend to apply for a licence to train on the Flat. I will have four two-year-olds and three three-year-olds in this yard by November 1. Please tell me if my application is likely to succeed." In this way you should not end up in the unenviable position of having rented a place, bought tack, and got owners and staff, only to find that in the following January your application is turned down.

At this stage we should look into the chance of becoming a private trainer, because if this crops up, you should grasp it with both hands. Most of a trainer's worries are financial ones: how to pay the fodder bills, how to pay the transport, how to pay the rent, etc. But if you are a private trainer, you can forget that side. Provided you can live on a salary plus 10 per cent of winning stakes, you have only to worry whether you get the sack at the end of your contract, or your employer dies or gives up owning racehorses. Of course, in these circumstances you will be out of a job, but as you have not had to find any cash, you are only back to square one, and you are in a far better position than if you had launched out on your own as a public trainer.

To return to the more probable situation, which is to start up as a public trainer, your next job after finding the stables is to collect some good owners. This is easier said than done and you will find that in order to get those seven young horses safely in the yard before you apply for a licence, you will take on anybody and will be truly thankful at the time. There are good owners and bad owners; and it is surprising how the new trainer can meet the bad before he finds the good.

There are a few folks owning racehorses today (and have been in the past for that matter) who are in the game simply for what they think may be easy money. These are the people who will often approach a new trainer, because they know full well he is desperate to fill his yard and will therefore be inclined to take their horse at a reduced fee.

Sometimes they remove their horse or horses from their present trainer, to whom they owe a considerable amount of money in fees, and tell the new man how badly the other man trains, etc. Very often the new trainer is forced to take on this sort of owner and therefore starts with a handicap. He will probably upset his fellow trainer by taking the owner, especially if the horses improve, though if this is not the case, the odds are that the horses will be removed as soon as the bill gets large enough to warrant it! However, "beggars can't be choosers" and therefore you may find that some of your first owners are in this category.

It is probable, however, that you will have at least one person who has promised to have horses with you and whom you know as a good friend. If luck is with you and your reliable owner remains alive and solvent, it is possible in time to form a stable of similarly sound people, who will trust you; in turn you will know you can trust them. When this is accomplished, you can heave a big sigh of relief, because even if training is a non-paying concern, you will at least know that monthly bills will be paid almost by return of post, and if one of your owners goes on a winter cruise, he will see you are paid and not left for three months to pay out continually with nothing coming in.

When trying to gather these essential first owners, you are likely to come across a person who like yourself is a new-comer; but whereas you have some experience of racing, even if not as a licensed trainer, he often has none about ownership. This can lead to a "knowledgeable" friend (about whom I have written elsewhere) being brought in, and this is very often the end of what could have been a good relationship.

The new owner whose approach is — "I have a bit of money to spend on racing as a hobby and I will leave it entirely to you to advise me and to see that I don't go broke" — is more likely to remain with you for life, than the one who says nothing and brings a friend to do the negotiations. The friend is invariably the type who has "little enough knowledge to be a dangerous thing"! He will poke his nose into the corn bin when he hopes you are not looking, though unless he saw a rat in it he would be none the wiser as regards the quality of the crushed oats. He will jump up and down on the gallops, rather as a house-agent tests a floor, but will know nothing about the going. Worse still, he will quiz the lads and folk in the local pub as to what sort of a bloke you are.

Although trainers have always been reluctant to emulate other businessmen and produce a "bill of fare", I am not sure they are right. It seems logical to have a printed document to hand out to a new owner, telling him exactly what he is expected to pay and what you are prepared to do for him. In this way, he can go home, digest the details and know how he stands. Perhaps some trainers do this nowadays, but I doubt if it is a general rule. If it is to be done on paper, it needs to be a sensible document drawn up with legal advice. By this I mean, supposing you put the new apprentice on a £10,000 yearling and he falls off and lets the horse loose up the main road. How do you stand if your owner sues for damage to his property if the horse meets a bus head-on and is killed? Your insurance may cover these things, but it will need a lot of argument to prove in court that the lad you had put up to ride the horse at exercise was competent to do so. A clause in your brochure stating "I am not responsible for any accidents etc. etc." might possibly put you in the clear.

A trainer starting up has all these points to consider, whereas when his owners become old friends, he knows that if there is a disaster he is unlikely to be sued for something which is probably an act of God.

Take, for example, the case of a trainer who in order to save his owner's cash, turns a horse out in a paddock from

June 1 until August 1. If the grass is good, there is no reason
why the horse should not stay out at night. The trainer makes
makes sure there is water in the paddock and either he or one
of his men visits the horse every afternoon. One night there
is a clap of thunder and one flash of lightning, unheard by
everyone except the horse, who gallops off in fright and gets
horribly tangled in a barbed-wire fence. The horse is found
dead at 3pm next day and has been dead for several hours.

In a case like this an awkward owner can "throw the book"
at you. It will be your fault all the way down the line; yet
you were only trying to help in the first place.

Further disasters can happen in the horse-box. Your
insurance will no doubt cover an accident, and possibly the
horses are insured; but this is not always the case. Some
owners do not insure, and supposing your driver comes into
a bend too fast, the horse falls down and breaks a leg? How
do you stand if the awkward owner sues you for killing his
£5,000 horse?

It is best that when you start training and collecting owners,
you should consider every way to protect yourself — just in
case you get one of the awkward squad. But let's hope you
can still find a few sporting types who have become owners
to enjoy their racing as a sport.

3

Employing Staff

At the present time racing is undergoing a crisis regarding stable labour. There is not only a shortage of labour but, I am sorry to say, the labour we have is not so good as it should be.

Many suggestions and ideas have been published, but to date nothing really encouraging has been put forward. We all know that stable lads are not well paid, but then neither are their employers.

Some agricultural workers are now paid far less than stablemen; yet for years they enjoyed an equal wage. The farming industry is just as important as the racing industry, so why should racing lads get more? Both of these trades are as important as some of those which command another £10 or £15 a week — and so it goes on.

It seems to me that any industry, unless it is nationalised (and so you and I suffer the loss) must cut its cloth to suit the coat. If you pay out 25 per cent more than you are taking in, you go out of business, no matter how kind-hearted you feel towards your staff.

Whereas most industries have a wide range of young people to choose from, racing is very restricted in this way. Firstly, it needs skilled labour of a specialised sort, and secondly this labour should not have a body-weight of over 9st. when fully developed. This naturally narrows the field, and although a vast increase in wages might easily attract more labour of a sort into racing, it would very likely consist of navvies off the M.1. motorway entirely unsuited to riding the Derby favourite at exercise!

Fortunately for all of us, the racing authorities fully understand that something must be done to keep young people coming in, and that something must be done to train them and keep them in the job, in order to teach the next generation. We will no doubt survive the crisis, but I will stick my neck out by saying that it can only be done by creating a situation whereby trainers are encouraged to take on apprentices, and the boys themselves are encouraged to come into racing.

One or, I hope, all three of the following ideas could help:—

(a) Weights in races should be raised to a minimum of 8st.

(b) Apprentice indentures should be altered and brought up to date.

(c) Trainers should not have to pay a full National Health Insurance stamp for apprentices.

Having sorted that lot out, we can consider the best way for a new trainer, with seven to ten young horses, to pick his staff.

The head-man is the key person, and in the same way that a subaltern is dependent on his sergeant to produce an efficient troop the trainer has to lean on his head-man. To continue this comparison, the capable officer who knows his job does not need quite such a good sergeant as the one who is still a bit "green". So when you select your head-man, you want to be sure what sort of man you need. If, for instance, you have not had a lot of experience in actual stable work and don't know how to dress over, muck out, feed, clip, give a drench or a physic ball etc., you are better off with an older man who does know. If, on the other hand, you know the job from A to Z, a young man who will do as he is told, is the better choice.

My father considered it was bad policy to take on a man older than yourself. His reasons were simply that if you were a good employer, your staff would stick with you; in turn when your employees got past their job, you would have to pension them off and leave them to occupy your cottage free of rent until they died. I know that in these days of the Welfare State this situation hardly applies; but at the same time, if your new head-man is 55-years-old, you must consider how good he will be at riding out in ten years time.

Whether you settle for a young man or an old one, and whether you are going to do the teaching or let the head-man do it, your next move should be to take on a lad or a girl, and teach them your methods. There will never be a better opportunity to do this than when you first start, since this is usually a time when you are still unlicensed and you will be at home most of the week. Also there is a lot more spare time to teach lads with seven horses in the yard than with seventy.

Michael Beary used to tell me that when he started training, late in life, his head-man, on receiving an order of which he did not approve, would say with a shrug — "Well, I suppose every trainer has his own methods." It was no doubt annoying to hear, but it is still very true, and if you can get those methods, which are to be yours for life, instilled into your staff, you have made a very good start.

The apprenticing of a boy, or for that matter taking on a girl, at the school leaving age of 16 is a subject which I am sure will be thoroughly gone into by the time you read this book.

You will have read so much about slave labour, cheap labour, sweated labour etc. that you will have a guilty complex before you start to employ anyone in your stable! However, one consolation is that none of this stuff is written by anybody who has an idea of what really goes on. You will read sensational articles, ghosted for the Sunday papers on behalf on an ex-jockey or unsuccessful stable lad, but you have to realise that for the money offered, it must be sensational. This is why invariably the trainer who did the alleged brutality is long since dead; likewise the owner who has told his jockey to stop his horse countless times will not be there to answer back. You won't read of any hardships which can be substantiated. However, just in case there is some truth in the yarns we read, I will try to explain how you set about apprenticing your first stable lad and jockey — and looking at it from the boy's angle, what he expects from you in return.

It is a great advantage if the lad in question (straight from school) has been to a riding school or had some previous experience; but this unfortunately is seldom the case, although girls seem more likely to have done so.

Parents will bring the boy and you will show them around your stables, show them where the boy will sleep, introduce them all to your head-man and any other boys you have at this early stage. You will agree with the boy and his parents that you will take him on a month's trial, and that if he feels at any time he is unsuited or you are convinced he will not be suited, the boy will be sent home at your expense. If after a month he still is not sure whether to sign on, give him longer until he is certain.

Meanwhile, you must consider this so-called slave-labour problem in its true light.

The lad who at 16 years of age weighs only 6st. is a likely prospect as a jockey, provided he does not start growing. A good look at the size of Dad and Mum, and a further glance at the boy's feet and hands, will give you a clue here — although in these times of long hair and both sexes wearing tight jeans, it is easy to make mistakes. I remember once the parents of a rather ungainly looking boy brought with them a much lighter and more agile child, and after my usual good look at the size of their respective feet and hands, I asked: "Why don't you let me have the other chap? He looks far more of a jockey." I was told sharply by the mother: "That's his elder sister!"

It is essential that the boy's school report be looked at, although some of them want careful study. I read in one report, "Excels in craft", which seemed to be the only good thing said. It was only after employing the boy for a year during which time he had "nicked" nearly everything on the place, including the head-lad's Christmas wage packet, that I began to suspect what the schoolmaster was trying to tell me!

Once, the boy, parents and Guv'nor have decided on a month's trial, it becomes a matter of giving encouragement and unlimited patience. The boy will be scared stiff of horses, and even if he has been to a riding school, he won't find one of your cheeky yearling colts quite the same as Old Dobbin. So, for a long time to come, he is not fit to enter a horse's box on his own, either to feed the horse or to tie it up in order to muck out or groom it. Likewise, for an even longer time, perhaps six months, he will not be safe to ride out one of your newly-acquired treasures.

The only way to teach him the stableman's job is to take him with you or your head-man and show him over and over again what to do, and then to allow him to practice when you are there to see he is doing the job properly. So many boys, especially in a busy yard, are left to get on with it, and then are cursed if things go wrong. But a new trainer with a small string has a much better chance to teach the lad.

The riding side can be done with the aid of a pony or very quiet hack. If these are not available, it is a good plan to arrange with the boy to meet your string as it returns from exercise about one mile from home, and then to allow him to ride one of the horses back to the yard. I found that this form of riding lesson acted as an intelligence test too. The new apprentice, unless he has his head screwed on, usually gets hopelessly lost trying to find the meeting place. I had one who was brought back by the police four hours later! Although there is no need for a high standard of education, jockeys do need to be mentally alert.

I remember a family from Lancashire arriving at my yard. The father, who brought his extremely sleepy looking son to greet me, apologised by saying: "I'm sorry but our John is a bit slow." I assured him that sometimes the slow ones turned out best in the end, and he turned and shouted over his shoulder: "We are all right Ma. He likes 'em slow." I couldn't say "no" after this sort of faith, but Dad was right and it took a very long time to get any useful service out of "our John".

It is a good plan to take on two boys at the same time, in spite of the extra cost. One lad on his own gets all the extra chores (which he must expect during the time he can't pull his weight). He also is very lonely, and a mate of the same age helps considerably.

Unlike school leavers who for about eight years have been at a boarding school, most boys have never been away from home, except perhaps to stay with an aunt or grandmother. It is no wonder they feel lost and homesick in their new surroundings.

I think a two-year interval is about right before you take on further apprentices. When you do, you are well advised to have your two original ones in the office and address them thus: "Now, you two boys have been here for two years and are beginning to learn the job and will possibly become jockeys. You have not been bullied by anyone and I want to be quite sure you give these new boys every chance to settle down and learn the job in the same way you have done. Any complaint from either new boy and I will be down on you like a ton of bricks.''

This sort of chat to your senior apprentices will cut out anything beyond the usual forms of horse-play, which is almost inevitable, and provided you are equally frank with the new boys, telling them that you will not tolerate bullying from the older boys and that it must be reported, all will be well.

The economics of employing apprentices is far more complex than paying your head-man or any other paid help. Each area more or less conforms to a pattern as regards paid labour, and if you try to pay less than your neighbour, you may deservedly lose your staff. However, apprentices are a different proposition, although as I have mentioned, I feel a change for the better will soon take place.

During the lad's trial period you do not pay his N.H.I. stamp. The boy is *not* employed and if the Ministry insists on payment, fight it with them, as I have done. Once he is signed on, you do pay — in full.

The cost of board and lodging is so much related to circumstance that it is almost impossible to assess. However, one hint which I can pass on is that it is far better to cope with them yourself on your own doorstep than to board them out in the town or a village pub. It may cost you more, but it is worth it. Whilst boys are apprenticed, they are your responsibility, not Mrs. Jones' down the road, who is charging £5 plus per week per head.

If you can manage to keep the boys on the premises, you should provide a decent dormitory or bedrooms, with the sort of bed-space that the Army or a hospital would not be ashamed of. The days of packing ten boys into a barn or hay-loft have long since gone. They now also need a decent living-room complete with heating and T.V., and an up-to-date plumbing set-up with bathroom and lavatory. Table tennis, bar billiards etc. are all a help.

Sheets, pillow cases, mattresses and beds are all very much with us too these days — and so they should be.

On my reckoning, the cost, including N.H.I. stamp for an under 18-year-old, is approximately a minimum of £12 per boy, taking into account clothing such as jeans, jodhpurs, boots, shoes, shirts, suits etc, and a share of electricity, laundry, coal or coke, caterers' wages etc.

We then have that most important and debatable point of pocket money to think about. In days gone by this sum was remarkably small, but that was at a time when a private soldier only received 7 shillings a week, provided he saluted smartly at the pay desk. It was therefore not such a crime for racehorse trainers to pay lads as young as 12 years of age only 2s. 6d a week. It was not meanness on the trainer's part, as much as assessing a sensible sum for a very young lad to spend on sweets or cigarettes when all else was found.

A boy at Eton aged 14 to 15 was, and is still for that matter, in the same position. How much should he be given, and how much would his parents like him to receive? Once one looks at an apprentice as a student or a learner, with everything found for him, and realises that this is the position for at least two years, one can look at the whole matter in the right perspective.

In other trades which entail apprenticeship, there seems to be no fair comparison. A boy who is sent to the local garage owner, plumber, or builder, usually lives at home, works for a set period (say from 9am to 5pm five days a week) and receives a wage. His N.H.I. stamp will be shared with his employer, just as a paid man's is in a racing stable. To compare this sort of apprenticeship with racing is not only unfair, but blatantly stupid. Of course the trainer would pay a decent wage, even if the boy is useless to him at the time, but how does he do that on top of a minimum outlay of £12 per week? The truth of the matter is that today none of our larger stables is employing apprentices at all. We have stables with over 100 horses that employ as few as *two* apprentices. This is not so much due to lack of applicants but to a disinclination on the trainers' part (a) to risk valuable bloodstock with such inexperienced staff, and (b) to be bothered to run a sort of prep-school with no fees coming in for the pupils!

Having pointed out that employing apprentices is by no means the road to fortune which those unacquainted with the trainer's cares are so apt to tell us, I still stress that if you are a reasonably young man and intend to make training your life, you must concentrate on teaching apprentices. Even if you go broke in your efforts, you will at least have trained some skilled staff for the benefit of racing's future, though you are not able to reap the profit yourself.

4

Economics

It is now time to put down on paper how much it is costing to keep each horse, before deciding how much you are going to charge your owners.

Without going into a lot of detail, you will find that to feed and bed down one horse will cost approximately £10 per week.

A racehorse is a convenient creature when it comes to assessing how much it will cost in fodder, because on average 1cwt each of hay, oats and straw will be used, even if there is a certain amount of wastage. On an average price one will pay through a hay and corn merchant, the following scale seems about right:—

1cwt oats, at £80 per ton	—	£4.00
1cwt hay, at £80 per ton	—	£4.00
1cwt straw, at £30 per ton	—	£1.50
	Total	£9.50

Then there is bran, linseed and vitamins etc, which means that £10 for fodder per horse per week is not far out.

To pay one man's wages and your share of N.H.I. stamp will cost at least £30, even if the man does not take as much home in his wage packet. You should work on the assumption that one man does two horses, not three or four. If you are to have your horses exercised in two lots, you need one man to two horses; and since lads may be off work through sickness or away with a horse, you will still find you have a third lot at exercise and your lads will often be doing three horses at night.

Adding these two major costings together, you arrive at the following:—

Keep of 1 horse per week	—	£10.00
Cost of half one lad's wages	—	£15.00
	Total	£25.00

Alarming though the figure may be, it becomes far more so when you take into consideration all the overheads; and the fewer horses in a yard with 30 boxes the greater share each one is responsible for. Rent will be £1,000 per annum at the least; telephone costs (for business purposes only) will be not less than £300 per year; heating and electricity (for lads only) will be £400 a year; laundry, bedding, repairs of damage, catering expenses, tack repairs, rates, water rates etc. will total at least £1,200 a year. A tenth share of approximately £3,000 means each horse in your yard must find £300 a year extra (approximately £6 per week), which will bring the total weekly expense to around £31 per horse. You then have to think about a profit out of which you can live.

Supposing you are not greedy and hope to live on the same wage as your head man, you will need to make at least £30 per week. This means a further £3 added to each horse's charge in your ten horse yard, taking the total to a £34 per week charge. Even then I am afraid you will still not make a profit; but it is important to be adamant that you will not train for less.

You may lose horses to the neighbour who is "under-cutting", but at least you will have the satisfaction of knowing he will be losing cash at the rate of £2 or £3 per horse per week.

In the days when all trainers charged 4 gns a week (or 5 gns at Newmarket), they paid their lads 45 shillings a week. To arrive at a training fee they merely doubled the cost of a man's pay, and hoped to make 10 shillings a week profit per horse. Old-time trainers were no more stupid or greedy than modern trainers, so if you take a leaf out of their book, you should charge £60 per week!

To continue on the important item of economy, we should look into the debatable question of a minimum charge to the owner, made compulsory by payment through Messrs Weatherby.

Although one gets the impression this is another recent brainwave, it has been discussed amongst trainers for at least 20 years, and possibly for longer. In principle, like so many schemes, it is sound, but in practice I for one cannot see it ever being enforced.

Take the example of a well-to-do farmer who has a few racehorses in training locally. He goes out of his way to grow first-class clover and rye grass hay and the best oats, untreated with chemicals either from the ground or from polishing etc. He then offers his products to his friend the trainer, who is delighted to buy good fodder, which he knows all about (he has probably seen it grown and harvested). The next move is an obvious one, namely that owner and trainer work on a barter basis. A £40 load of hay may pay for one horse and a £80 load of oats for two others. Now, how on earth are Messrs Weatherby expected to sort out that type of amicable agreement?

A trainer desperate to get more horses often "under-cuts" by charging less. But how will a compulsory fee of, say, £35 a week stop him? He can easily hand back a tenner to the owner and who is to know?

These are just two reasons which we realised years ago would prevent what sounded a good scheme from ever being feasible, and there are several more. Although Major General Sir Randle Feilden was ridiculed for his famous remark about not inquiring into how much "Jeremy" paid his butler, as far as I am concerned he was quite right, and as usual dead on target!

Racing has been handed down to us as a privately-run sport, and although it has now also become an industry, it is still basically a private sport. A person who can afford a private servant – such as a groom, butler, cook, gardener or chauffeur pays by mutual agreement, not by a union rate or by any other form of compulsion. A private trainer must rank along with any other private servant, and the latter's staff, one would logically suppose to be on the same footing.

As staff in a private yard is identical to staff in a public trainer's yard, and the trainer is carrying out an identical trade, how can one start to dictate how much the owner pays the trainer in either case? Likewise, nobody is forced to keep an account with Messrs Weatherby, any more than he is forced to bank with Lloyds. So there can be no sort of compulsion, as far as I can see, for owners to pay a minimum fee through Weatherbys.

Racehorse owners are repeatedly told there is no need for them to own horses – and they are usually told this when they have the audacity to ask for a more realistic first prize than their grandfathers were reluctant to accept. But there may come a day when the long-suffering owner tires of being criticised and bullied, and quits his expensive hobby altogether. Then where will we be? For a long time the owner has been brought down from "No. 1 in the charts" and is now about No. 10, well behind punters, stable lads, racing journalists and Co. However, to a new trainer the owner must be No. 1, and you won't make a living from training if you think otherwise.

Your duty is to your owner and his horse, and if you stick to that resolution, you can rest assured that although "the little dogs bark, the caravan will still go on".

Nobody who has trained horses, or no chartered accountant who does a trainer's work, will deny that it has become virtually impossible to show a profit on the keep of each horse. Again this is nothing new; it has been the case for the last 30 years. But what has made matters worse for the trainer is the fact that ordinary stake money has not increased in relationship to the cost of living, buying fodder, and paying staff.

If we admit that a trainer cannot make a small profit per horse, we must look into other ways he can keep in business. It is a rule of racing that he will receive 10 per cent of winning stakes from the owner; and personally I think he should receive 10 per cent of place money too, but this is not uniform. It is also usual procedure for either the owner or buyer of a horse sold out of the yard to give the trainer a rake-off.

These are the only two sure sources of income, apart from the running of your own horse-box and a large monthly turnover, which although not income, does help a lot with a "robbing Peter to pay Paul" procedure.

The only other hope is betting, unless you take on another business altogether such as farming, though trainers find they have quite enough to do to run the one job.

Betting has always been a dicey way of making a living, and from a trainer's point of view it has never been harder than it is today. The competition is so much greater, and from what I can see bookmakers are far more cautious.

We have now arrived at a situation whereby trainers earning £30,000 a year for their owners and receiving £3,000 for themselves should be able to get by. But for the 85 per cent who are earning well under £10,000 in winning stakes it is indeed a struggle. One thousand pounds is less than you are paying your lads, and £10,000 in stake money takes a lot of earning if you have a small yard.

Only a few years ago I won 17 races with only 15 horses in the yard, and my 10 per cent came to £450. This small fortune was made by winning highly-competitive two-year-old races, which was all I could do as most of my horses were of that age.

There are, of course, steps to be taken as regards economy. One can cut the labour, which I am afraid will be the first move when the lads' wages increase.

All this does is to make your stable less efficient and to upset your good lads by over-facing them.

You can believe what you have read about employing apprentices, but as I have pointed out it is not just cheap labour.

You can try to cut down on fodder, but although race-horses are convenient in how much they consume, they insist on the best grub in order to win races, so that will not work.

The irony of training fees is that whereas men at the top who are earning £5,000 and more from winning stakes can charge the maximum fee, the man who is lucky to earn £1,000 a year must charge far less in order to get owners.

I am sorry that in this chapter on economics I can only point out the losses, and have no constructive ideas as to how to balance the budget.

As we are today, the policy seems to be, "Let the rich get richer and the poor get poorer". However, as the vast majority are in the poorer bracket, it seems only a matter of time before the pendulum swings to help the small men. Otherwise it will mean a dozen trainers, and a handful of millionaires as owners, will control racing, and that will bore us all.

5

Breaking Yearlings

A trainer who has collected a few yearlings by October and is hoping for his licence to be granted in January has as good a chance to break in those youngsters as he has to teach his new apprentices. In fact, he will never have a better chance if his hopes are fulfilled and the stable increases its numbers each year.

To break a yearling — and I am not sure this expression gives the right idea — is still the same business our grand-fathers carried out 100 years ago. We have the same problems, the same risks, and the same adequate results.

Other types of horsemen have different ideas. Cowboys in some parts of the world tether the horse to a tree and let it learn the hard way, with a semi-stranglehold on its throat. Hunting people and anyone other than racehorse trainers take a very long and steady view of the whole proceeding. They usually do the job inside a stable, and not out in the open as racing folk do.

There is one major factor in the breaking process which causes an "explosive" reaction on the horses part, which is the tightening of any sort of strap around its girth.

In racing we first teach the horse to lunge both ways with a bit in its mouth, with one long rein attached and a cavesson on top of the bridle with another rein attached to the nose.

We then come to putting on a breaking roller, a simple contraption which has a belt around the chest and a girth to

tighten around the horse's belly. In addition there are two
buckles on the front of the roller to take side reins, which
buckle into the rings of the bridle, and a fitting at the rear to
take a tail crupper.

It is when we tighten the belly strap that the trouble starts
and our yearling explodes. Once that constriction around the
middle is felt, the horse will start a series of buck jumps, just
as we see in a rodeo act, where a kicking strap is applied
further back in the flanks. It is this first series of high jumps,
landing with fore-legs dead straight, on possibly hard or
uneven going, which is the peak of the danger period. But
unless we change the approach to the whole system, which
I think is long overdue, we must carry on as grandfather did
and hope for the best.

I have already published my ideas on breaking yearlings and
in a nutshell, all I think is important is to do this tightening
around the belly as soon as the foal is born, in just the same
way that studs have learned to put a head collar on a foal and
to lead it to and from the paddock. John Hislop tried this
out on Brigadier Gerard's younger sister and when the filly
was tacked as a yearling, she went around the lunging reins
without any jumps and plunges. In view of this, I think with
enough patience we could all do it, even at yearling stage, by
very quietly tightening the girth inch by inch, instead of
doing it all in one movement and inducing the hi-jinks, often
on unsuitable ground.

However, if we are to carry on as our ancestors did,
bearing in mind that the yearling is valuable and not to be
injured, the drill is approximately as follows:—

It is essential to find some good yielding going, though
that, in September and October is not easy, unless you can
find a stubble or some plough. You only need a bit of ground
about the size of a tennis court. Then, according to the fitness
of the yearling, we spend a few days teaching it to circle

around on the lunging reins, one on the nose and the other attached to the bit with a "coupling", so that there is equal pressure on both sides. If the yearling is fit and obviously ready to stand plenty of exertion, three days' lunging is enough. If it is very fat and over-fed, as many bought at auction are, you must keep it on the rein far longer, until you feel it is up to strenuous exercise.

I think there is a lot of damage done each year to some of the most expensive purchases by suddenly subjecting them to a bout of violent exercise. In his own interests, the breeder and seller has to produce the yearling in the best possible condition for the sales. He likes to see it looking well in condition, and the last month before the sale of a yearling for which 10,000 guineas is expected is a worrying time. If the horse is left to run out every day in the paddock as it has been doing, there is always the risk of a last-minute injury. The breeder is in much the same position as a trainer whose horse is favourite for a valuable race. Fate, being as fickle as we know it to be, seems invariably to decide that the best horse is the one who meets bad luck at the worst time. It is hard for you as a purchaser to know exactly how much exercise the yearling has taken during the past month, but you are well advised to work on the assumption that it has been having the "wrapped in cotton wool treatment", especially if its coat is very sleek and there appears to be more than the usual meat on the ribs, back and neck.

When one has only a few yearlings to break and decent weather for the job, there is no need to hurry. The more you handle the yearling, lunging it both ways, leading it on both sides etc., the less trouble it will be to break. It is interesting that a horse which has been brought up on the place from birth, and has confidence in the folk which it knows, is far easier to deal with than a newcomer.

When the main danger period is over and the roller has been

put on for the first time, the next rather hazardous task is to get a rein or rope tied or held around the horse's rump. We usually tie a piece of strong webbing or rope from the offside of the roller, pass it around under the tail, making sure that it will not fall below the hocks, and secure it to the near-side of the roller. The object is to get the yearling used to a rein touching its flanks and hind legs before we try to drive it in long reins.

Again I am not sure grandfather was right in this method. Once one has adjusted this strap and the yearling feels the pressure, it invariably scampers around at a rate of knots with violent kicks, when it finds time to deliver them, to get rid of this tail string. I found it was safer to fix the rein, as before, on the far side of the roller, but to keep the other end in my hand, so that if the horse was really upset, I could let go and start again. In this way, you avoid being unable to break off the fight if it gets beyond reason. I have seen a few horses, usually fillies, who would not stand for the rein around their quarters, and after hair-raising experiments, I gave in and never drove them in long reins. Strangely enough, after these fillies had been ridden for some time and an exercise sheet put on, they did not mind the tail string, which after all was the reason for all the fuss in the first place.

A very good filly of my father's called Dented Bell (who won six good two-year-old races and became a successful broodmare) was one of the sort described; and I am sure that if we had not had a sharp knife handy to cut short the rein around her rump, she would have seriously damaged herself. As it was, we merely rode her without any driving and she had a perfect mouth and temperament.

This brings us to driving in long-reins, and whether it is essential or not. When you have time to make as good a job as possible of breaking in a few yearlings, it is certainly a wise move; but if you have 30 or more yearlings to break between

August and October, I don't see how it can be done. Furthermore, if it is done in the latter circumstances, I doubt whether the horse benefits.

So much depends on the man who does the driving. A stable lad who has not had a lot of experience with long reins is not the person to do it. Neither is your riding school expert, since he or she does not have the same approach. A racehorse has the same mouth as any other sort of horse, but for him it must be fashioned to "pull" and not to "drop the bit", which is the aim in other forms of riding. Therefore, one has to teach the yearling racehorse to go into his bridle and at the same time not to be afraid of doing so. To do this one has to be gentle on the mouth but at the same time far harder on it than is required by other forms of horsemanship.

Our yearling needs to get used to quite a lot of pressure on its tender mouth, and the shorter jockeys try to ride, I am afraid the greater that pressure will become. To drive a yearling in long reins for racing purposes one needs to encourage it all the time to take hold of the bit. This can be done by walking more slowly than the horse, making it give you a slight "tow" on your steady journey. Changing direction of the lunging is also very useful, and when one gets used to "taking in the spare" without having the long reins all over the place, it is a lesson well taught, but not so important as that vital lesson which is far better imparted by a good rider than a driver, and that is to go into the bridle.

Whether you drive the horse or not, you must still come round to the day when you ride it.

When I spent a short spell with Noel Murless, the time from first putting on the tack to the yearling being ridden away was remarkably short. As far as I remember about three days sufficed, and "the proof of the pudding is in the eating". Murless has had very little trouble during the last 20 years as regards the mouths of his horses, and his record speaks for itself.

The trouble I noticed with rushed breaking was invariably sore girths. In order to avoid a battle with the horse on the second day of putting on the tack, one is inclined to leave the roller on all day and perhaps over-night, which will inevitably cause a sore girth. The horse has sweated during its exertions and unless we remove all traces of sweat and dirt a sore place will certainly form. This "chafe" as it is called, is very painful, and a horse who would otherwise walk quietly out of the yard will be inclined to become difficult if it is in pain and discomfort.

The trainer with unlimited time can take the roller off the horse after the first session, sponge away the sweat marks and dry thoroughly. The next day may mean another bucking exhibition, but he will at least be saved the sore-girth problem. He can go on slowly, replacing the roller with a saddle on the third day, then driving the horse for at least seven days. Then, as it returns to the stables, he can put a boy across the horse's withers in the loose box. This is a good opportunity to make use of your new apprentice. He will no doubt think he is taking his life in his hands, but in fact he is only doing the job of a dummy or a sack of sand. The horse at this stage is not concerned about how good the rider is, but is merely having an introduction to accepting weight on its back. Trainers usually carry out this procedure in the horse's stable and it is rare that any trouble occurs.

In 99 cases out of a 100 a yearling very soon allows the rider to sit upright in the saddle and ride him around the box. However, I remember when I was about 13 years old and was used regularly for this job, I encountered a French-bred colt who had been a lot of trouble from the start. No sooner had I been lifted across the horse's neck for the initial stage, than the horse went beserk. We all landed in a heap in a corner of the box and the horse remained on the floor. He had hit his head an almighty blow on the wall of the box and had fractured his skull.

Once the new apprentice has got used to his daily rides around the box supervised by yourself or head man, and about seven days driving have taken place, it is time to get out in wide-open spaces. It is also time to replace the new apprentice with a more-experienced rider. There is an old saying amongst trainers that it is wrong to put two novices together, and it holds good for schooling jumpers, riding in two-year-old races and riding yearlings on their first outing. The better the horseman at this stage the more he will teach your horse. It is a comparatively simple job to teach a yearling, and anyone who has had plenty of practice will, in only a few rides, teach the horse enough for it to be a simple ride for anyone else. It is yearlings who have been started with poor riders, possibly more frightened than they are, which become a trouble. I would sooner see a 10st jump jockey ride the yearling for ten minutes only, than a 6st boy who will fall off, frighten it, and teach it bad habits.

Once the riding stage is reached a narrow drive or grass lane with high hedges on each side is a great asset. In this way, the yearling is forced to keep a straight course and is less likely to lose its rider than if an open field is used. Provided there is not too much traffic, the road is therefore a better starting place than a paddock, and a yearling, especially if it is still unshod behind, will jump around less on the hard surface of the road.

6

Two-Year-Olds

A trainer who has just started up on the Flat will inevitably find himself with a stable consisting mainly of two and three-year-olds. This is, of course, for a license to train on the Flat.

Assuming you have six two-year-olds in a stable of 12 horses and that it is January, we can discuss how you are to train these youngsters. There is no doubt that training a two-year-old is a different job from training any other horse in the yard. Every trainer will have different ideas and a vast number will have had more success than I, so I can only try to convey ideas which I learned from my father and some which I worked out for myself by trial and error.

The first rule I learned is almost a first commandment: "Treat the two-year-old like a child." Once one has it firmly planted in one's head that from January 1 and through the first year's racing the two-year-old is the equivalent of a 12 to 14-year-old child, one has a good chance of being a successful trainer of two-year-olds. Some points that follow are:

(a)   Do not keep the horse out too long at exercise.
(b)   Do not put a heavy lad on it for too long.
(c)   Do not work it over any distance further than 5 furlongs until much later in the year.
(d)   Do not allow it to be hit in a race or gallop, or in its stable.

Two-year-olds, like any young animal, are playful, both in the box and at exercise. In correcting this "horse-play" a lot of harm is often done. If you give way to them all the time, they will get the upper hand; if you nag at them all the time, you will sour them and turn what started out as play into spite. It really needs confidence, which can only be gained from experience, to handle two-year-olds successfully. If you have only young apprentices or stable girls to cope, it means watching very carefully how they are getting on with their charges.

I remember a stallion, known to be very hard to handle, who arrived at a stud in Yorkshire, where he was put in the charge of a farm hand who had very little horse knowledge but a lot of confidence and was entirely without fear. At the previous stud, to exercise this horse had entailed two men and a chifney bit in its mouth; but when the farm labourer led the horse out on a bridle and merely responded to its rearing and striking out with, "Lay off it — you stupid boogar;" the stallion was so deflated by the lack of interest shown in his performance that for many years he became a very easy horse to deal with.

Another example of confidence, which after all is the basic principle of all horsemanship, concerns Sir Gordon Richards, who was engaged to ride a horse of my father's called Diagram at Brighton. Diagram was a very hard puller and Gordon realised he might end up in the sea instead of reaching the start; so he asked to be let off the ride but assured my father that Steve Donoghue would take his place. Steve, who was just recovering from an all-night Brighton session, knew nothing of Diagram's reputation and cantered down to the start as if he was riding the starter's hack!

It is this thought transference between groom or rider and horse which counts so much with two-year-olds. The older horse is more set in his ways and therefore harder to teach, but it is the early years which will have formed his character. Horses which have been handled properly from birth are by far the easiest to deal with later on.

Many trainers who have had care of high-class horses will confirm that as a rule these superbly-bred animals are far less difficult than lowly-bred types, and some of them put this down to good breeding alone. However, it is more likely that the high-class yearling comes into training after being handled by experts, while some of the lower-class horses often have had no handling at all. So possibly it is not the blue blood which counts, but a good early education.

Regarding preparation of the six two-year-olds and obeying the commandments laid down for the general treatment, you must now make your mind up which are to race early and which will need more time.

In the old days many trainers galloped their yearlings over three furlongs before Christmas. I remember Ernie Davey once telling me that he would win the Brocklesby. That was before January 1 — and he was right!

Once you have them cantering upsides and have taught them to take hold of the bit and to go straight, it cannot possibly hurt them to sprint for three furlongs. It is, after all, what they would do if they were still out in the paddock. The result of this little sprint can give some useful information, since you will see which have speed, an essential for a race horse. You will not know at this stage whether the speedy one will stay more than three furlongs, but the odds are that it will do so, if it has far more speed than the others.

The worst result in this early test is to have the whole bunch finish in line, which usually means that none of them can "go".

There is nothing like using an older horse, of known ability and ridden by a sensible rider, to keep things at the right level. If you take three juveniles with your three best riders and work them over the three furlongs, with either yourself or head man on the older horse, you can repeat the identical sprint a few days later with the next bunch. In this way, if you watch carefully, you should know (even in December) if you have an early winner in the yard.

Perhaps some trainers, especially the ones just starting up, may get over-keen at this stage. I remember one season when my three two-year-olds were obviously useless, but I would not admit it. In March I was trying, with the aid of Michael Beary, to persuade the slowest of the three to show some sort of speed, because the owner particularly wanted to run him at Chester in May. Michael suggested I crack the hunting crop behind him, hoping it might do the trick. I have never been very fleet of foot, but to my horror I overtook Michael and his mount within the first 100 yards of pursuit with the "long-tom" — and I was wearing a duffle coat and wellingtons too! Michael, who was a super-optimist as well as the best all-round horseman I have seen, assured us that the horse had given him "a great feel" and that it was sure to improve.

However, lack of speed is usually a true guide to the ability of a racehorse, and when I visited the late Gerald Balding's yard at Weyhill, I was shown the same horse, who was by then a four-year-old. Gerald said: "I am afraid he is not much good as a racehorse, but he should make a three-day event horse." His head-man Gerry Hamilton, who I am sorry to say is also dead, came out in his quiet Irish brogue with: "Ah, sure, that's what this fella' needs; he would never win any sort of event in one day!"

If you are lucky, you will find one yearling which in December, or as a two-year-old in January/February, stands out a mile. It really can "go" and you have seen it outpace a decent sprinter over three furlongs at approximately weight for age (3st. 7lb.) in early January. You must then decide whether to keep it for later in the year, or go to battle early and win a race. A lot depends on the class of horse you are dealing with.

If, for instance, a classic winner was galloped in the way I have suggested, I am sure he would mesmerise the others; but then one does not ask one's Classic hope to do early sprinting. Our charge is more likely to be an ordinary type, costing the average or less as a yearling, and for him I would say that the principle of a "bird in hand is worth two in the bush" is the right one.

The early racing of two-year-olds does not necessarily harm them, provided the trainer has his commandments in mind.

One can pause a minute and think about the high-class two-year-olds who are expected to win important races on their first outing. They cannot possibly do this without a number of "dress rehearsals". So it really boils down to two questions: Are you doing better to race the two-year-old with a good jockey up and on presumably the best going that can be produced; or are you doing better by galloping it at home, where possibly conditions may not be quite so good?

It is a difficult choice but I think when one reads "lightly-raced as a two-year-old", one really wants to know how many "races" it has had on the gallops, possibly being badly ridden on unsuitable ground, before one can assess any damage that may have been done. One should not take it for granted that the two-year-old who has run six or eight times has been over raced, whereas the one that has only run twice and won twice has been lightly-raced.

Some successful trainers of two-year-olds in the old days gave them a tremendous amount of fast work, and although it is hard for anyone — even another trainer — to know just what his neighbour does, I think the late Atty Persse used to put his youngsters through the mill more than his contemporaries. The results were definitely good, and one of Atty's running for the first time, knew the job. It would run as an arrow, whereas some of the opposition would run "green" and be beaten not so much by lack of ability as lack of racing knowledge.

It is certainly a point to consider with two-year-olds whether it is fitness which wins early races or whether it is the lesson of how to race which really counts. I think (but that is as far as I go) that the latter counts more, and if you have one good rider, he will teach your early two-year-old the job without having to gallop it more than twice. Two-year-olds and novice jumpers need the best and most experienced riders available to get the best out of them, but so often they are given the worst help from the saddle and then blamed for taking six months to learn a lesson which could have been digested in three minutes.

7

Developing a Method

Since every trainer has his own methods, it is hard for a
newcomer to know which are the best methods to copy.

In the same way that "Jack" Leader had a flair for picking
yearlings, some trainers have a flair for training and do their
job more by instinct than working to any sort of formula.

My father, Frank Hartigan, was at the top of his profession
for a long time, and I think that his record of winners has yet
to be broken. Whereas he was not a particularly good judge
of a yearling, his instinct as regards what work each horse
needed was incredible. If he had been blindfolded, I am sure
that simply by running his hand over a horse's back at stable
time, he would have known which of his 60 horses it was,
how fit it was and what work it needed next day. I remember
going round stables with him after he had been away for a
week, and when we came into one box, he said: "And what
the hell have you been doing to this poor horse while I was
away?" The horse in question had got loose two days before
and had completed about two miles on the gallops, but as it
had no scratches or any other ill-effects that we could see, we
had kept quiet about it. However, "the old man" had spotted
the effect of that extra "spin" as soon as he entered the box
and we had to own up.

He trained his horses entirely on the needs of each individual. There was no such thing as a work day on Tuesday,
Thursday and Saturday etc.; it was work every day for some

horses and a holiday on the leading rein for others. By carrying out this sort of programme he made it very difficult for himself, especially as he never took notes of which horses had cantered where or when.

We used to give linseed mash on Wednesday and Saturday, and as my father went round stables he would tell his head man: "Don't mash this one tonight"; and that would mean he had just decided to gallop it the following morning. He would take the head lad into the office after stables and make out the "list". This vital piece of information was then written in chalk on a slate by the head man and displayed in the tack place, but it was my father, not the head man, who decided which lad rode which horse.

When I started training, I naturally tried to carry on in the way I had been taught, but I found it was a great help to keep the previous night's copy of the list. Even if (as in my case) never more than 30 horses are involved, it is hard to remember exactly what you did three days ago with so and so, at the same time remembering when it is due for its next race. A couple of diaries are a good aid; one noting all the meetings and horses engaged, and the other with a complete record of each day's work.

Two other books are useful, the one an alphabetically indexed book with each horse's engagements kept up to date. This includes the date of the race, meeting, distance, date of four-day forfeit, cash involved, and ultimate stake, etc. This sort of book is nothing new and no trainer can work without it. My other book, which was identical to look at, was for keeping a check on the lads employed over the years. Perhaps some trainers do not bother with this one, but I found it very useful. Trainers are apt to give boys nicknames, and when they receive a letter from another trainer asking for a reference for "Albert Jones", it can become rather embarrassing, because Albert Jones may have been known to them as Bonzo, Sailor or Geordie. In five years time they will still remember him under his alias, but the name Albert Jones is unlikely to ring a bell unless he has been one of the very few successful apprentice jockeys. Keeping a lads' book is only a matter of minutes. When you first take on the lad, enter his full names, age, religion, next of kin, home address, previous jobs and date when he was first employed; on the day he leaves, make an entry of how and why he left, and a short report.

In the case of an apprentice, I found the book even more useful, because I would record such items as — "bought new jodhpurs 13. 7. 70"; "bought shirt and socks 10. 9. 70." etc. Also the final report can prove interesting in years to come. Here are some quotes:—

"Decent lad but very dumb and too heavy, eventually sent home after breaking the chaff cutter — following a two months trial period."

"Good stableman of the old school, but obviously only 'hibernating' in a small jump stable in order to return to Newmarket in the spring."

"Adequate jump jockey and box driver, sacked for flogging small apprentices, wife and horse-box — in that order!"

"A very decent boy, served five years and left to get married, is sure to stay in racing and will probably come back to me."

There is no end to my lads' book quotations and it is a heartening thought that amongst the hundreds in it, there are only two who left because they were dishonest. We are often given the impression that racing is a bit of a rogues' sport, but if this is so, it certainly does not apply to the lads, at least as far as my dealings with them have been. I never bothered to lock things up; I asked any of the lads to come in to baby-sit, feed the cats, or listen for the telephone, and I can't recall a single instance of petty theft or abuse of the trust I placed in them. It is just as well when you are formulating your methods to give particular attention to this trust relationship with your new apprentices.

Most trainers have a last look round at night to see that all is well in the yard and if they don't do it themselves, the head man steps in; but it is a wise move for either of you to take along the new apprentice. The boy will learn to look in the manger and see how the feed is going down, to look at the haynet and the water bucket, to adjust the rug if necessary and above all to see that the door is properly shut. If you do this for a few months, the boy should be capable of doing the job on his own and of coming in to report what he has found on his tour of the yard. It gives your apprentice confidence to think he is trusted to do such an important job — even if you have to sneak out later, to make sure that he has actually gone into Blank's box, as you know he is scared stiff of the horse. In principle it is a very good method and you will finish with an intelligent, reliable lad at the end of his time.

The final look round is very important and many a major disaster has been saved by it. The horse that is cast, or one that has managed to get its foot under the door when the bottom catch has been left off, or the horse with colic can become fatalities if left all night without aid. The boy who comes in at 9.15 p.m. and reports "All have eaten up, sir, apart from Blank who has not touched his feed," not only gets you away from T.V. or the form book to go and take Blank's temperature, but also learns a lot from how you go on from there. If the horse has a temperature of say 102°, you possibly go to your medicine chest and produce a syringe and dose of antibiotic. You explain to the lad what you are doing and why, and that if the temperature is still up in the morning, you will get the vet. It is this sort of opportunity put in a lad's way at a time when through no fault of his own he is still more of a liability than an asset, which will pay a dividend later on.

A job on the gallops in the afternoon, helping you to put in tracks or build a schooling fence, always with the reward of a few pence, is a far better method than ignoring the lad in his off-duty hours and paying him far more pocket money than is good for him at 16 years of age.

These days it is not only stable lads who don't wish to work any harder than necessary; it is all of us. So your ideas of what you and your head man expect should be made clear from the start, bearing in mind you should not expect any-thing like the work or the hours of work which took place years ago when racing's labour situation was far better. It is now a matter of sticking to the essentials. You will have made a start if, for example, you insist on a horse's feet being picked out and washed out every day, and that no sweat marks from the saddle or girths are left; but you will also have to give way on other points, such as a thorough dressing over. If you keep the lads till 12.30 in the morning, cleaning tack and sweeping the yard, you will have to let them off early on a wet day, when the horses cannot get out. Furthermore, you must realise that whatever the stable lads' wage is increased to, you will still be in the same boat.

Although I may have been of help in this chapter on developing methods as regards labour, I cannot help much on the horse's side. It is, as I have said, entirely up to the trainer himself whether he works by instinct or follows a definite pattern; but if you have not the "flair", it is far better to lay down a routine of work and stick to it, rather than try to do a mixture of both methods.

The late Charles Elsey told me he found it a great help to train the progeny of mares he had trained. I think there is a lot of truth in this, and the few horses I did train, following their dams, had very much the same characteristics regarding the work needed, their staying ability and their temperament and so on.

8

When Patience is Needed

We all recognise the truth of the saying "Patience is a virtue", but perhaps many people do not realise how important it is for a racehorse trainer to be patient, and also how in some circumstances it is difficult for him. The trainer who has a reputation for unlimited patience is often the successful one, but whether success follows his patience or he is so placed financially that he can afford to be patient, is another matter.

A trainer may be prepared to sit for hours on the river bank without catching a fish, but if by June he has not trained a winner, he can become very restless. When this happens, some of his good resolutions, made six months earlier, go by the board.

The most promising and best-bred two-year-old in the yard, whose first race was planned for September, often finds itself kicking off in July, in order to earn some cash and raise the stable's morale. The wealthy owner who has stressed there is no need to hurry the horse, and that he does not mind if the horse does not run as a two-year-old, will be told about a sudden improvement and of a complete change of plan. Sometimes in a case like this all is well and no harm is done, but there must be many backward horses, suddenly "wound up" after a long period of slow and steady work, who do suffer from this lack of patience on the trainer's part.

Since the days when the training charge showed a small profit, we have seen less and less of the patient trainer. It was not uncommon in those days for a horse to be kept in full training from its yearling days until midway through its four-year-old career. Then by winning a £1,000 stake it would pay for its keep for all those years.

It was certainly easier to be patient 30 years ago, but whether it all added up to better training and better horses is one of those comparisons which is impossible to make. It is similar to futile arguments such as whether Golden Miller was better than Arkle, or Gordon Richards better than Lester Piggott.

A great deal depends on the patient trainer's selection as to which particular horse he is going to give time. This is where the art lies. It is no good waiting two years with a horse which could have been winning races from its early two-year-old days. Yet how is one to know?

The size of the horse is one guide and the breeding another, but neither is a guarantee you are about to do the right thing. I think development means more than the actual height of the horse, and the performances of the dam and her previous foals give a better clue than ability of the sire and his offspring.

A yearling who stands 16.0 hands when bought in September may still be an early sort, provided it is furnished and not just long in the leg and back.

I once bought a yearling colt who was not foaled until June 20. He was a massive individual, standing 16.1 and built to carry 13st to hounds. It looked as if much time and patience would be needed, but he won his first race in the following May, when still not two years of age, and was placed on eight other occasions before he broke a leg as a three-year-old and had to be destroyed early in the season. I think the only reason this horse did not need time was because he had become fully grown and developed in a remarkably short time and also was bred purely to sprint.

It is the other sort, which are under-developed, who often

need time, and it is not necessarily their height which counts. A yearling under 15 hands may need a year before you can race him, but there are usually signs to look for. The amount of bone below the knee, the size of the head and feet, whether the quarters are slightly higher than the withers: they can all give you an idea as to how tall the horse will be when he is fully grown. You then have to realise it is hard to expect the horse to grow as much as one hand and also race at his best during the growing period.

The main difficulty is to find the right horse for the right owner. Your patient owner, who even at today's costs is prepared to bide his time, often ends up with a horse capable of winning in April. But as you are committed to giving it time, you may hang on until August before you run, only to find there are others of higher standard than you would have been able to defeat earlier in the year. Likewise, the impatient owner (if one can call anybody that, merely because he wishes to get as much fun out of his hobby as possible) may find he owns a horse who should not see a racecourse for 12 months. But in order to please him and keep him from moving his horses to another trainer, you will try to beat nature by running the horse far sooner than you should.

In both cases you will have done the wrong thing. Yet it is not altogether lack of patience on your part which has failed to earn you the reputation of being a patient trainer; circumstance has forced your hand, and lack of money is more often than not the motive which makes an otherwise patient man move a few months before he would otherwise have done so.

I had only one golfing lesson in my life and the only advice I can remember from the professional included the words "DO NOT PRESS". I discovered that this signified I was trying to hit the ball too hard. Pressing, I was told, meant

that my hurried, wild swipe at the ball was doomed to
failure, whereas a more patient, controlled effort would
possibly have kept me on the fairway. It is this "pressing"
which can spoil a trainer's chance of winning a race with a
horse he has planned to keep for later in the year. Things
may have gone against you early in the year. The stable may
have had the cough or a virus infection and by mid-summer
you are getting desperate. The wise and patient trainer will
stop running the horses until they are back to form, but often
one says to oneself, "Surely that race on Monday is a gift,
even if the horse is not bang in form". Such wishful thinking
usually means a further defeat and that the horse takes a long
time to recover. Bob Armstrong, after an unsuccessful trip
to Scotland, was apt to say, "Well, we must go home now,
mend our nets and cast them again nearer the shore." That
is the right attitude.

9

Good and Bad Horses

Although it is possible the new trainer will collect bad owners before he gets good ones, it is almost certain he will have to put up with bad horses before he has the thrill of knowing he has a really good one in his yard.

We read a lot about the number of bad horses in training, but if the folk who complain paused to think first, they would realise that what they mean is there are too many horses in training.

The fact that only one horse in five ever wins a race is unlikely to change, especially if it remains policy not to cater for the less good.

When the Bible states that, "Those who run in a race, run all, but one receives the prize," it sums up the situation very neatly.

If there are four bad horses to one good one (and in my opinion that is an underestimate), it is obvious that the more horses there are in training, the greater is the percentage of bad horses. So why folk grumble about today's situation I just cannot understand; especially as about 75 per cent of these so-called bad horses are sold to race abroad, where in their new surroundings they become good horses. The grateful purchasers send photographs back of the so-called bad horse standing in triumph with a garland of flowers around his neck and a coloured jockey up. Then you read to your amazement that it has won the equivalent of £3,000.

Surely it is all a matter of comparison; and once your horse has won a race he has become in your eyes a good horse — especially if its your first winner

Some trainers, in my opinion the best, make up their minds to win a race with every horse, no matter whether it's a seller in Scotland or a three-year-old hurdle at Newton Abbot. It is a challenge to get the horse first past the post, and having done so the trainer usually tells the owner that: "Lightning doesn't strike twice; now is the time to sell."

The main problem is to convince the owner that his horse is very moderate, without losing the owner. Obviously when you first get the horse, whether you have bought it for the owner or he has produced it, you tell him how much you like it and how good you think it could be. This is human nature, and if you do not show faith at this stage, you will not keep many owners.

It is the next stage which becomes difficult. Having painted this rosy picture without really knowing anything, how are you to break the news when at last you realise your swan is only a goose — and a slow one at that? I have always found that honesty is the best policy, and that "kidding" the owner to keep his horse in training, with a lot of blarney about how it will grow between two and three years of age and how the sun on its back will do a power of good, only loses you an intelligent owner. If your owner knows you are entirely straight and are thinking about his interests as much as your own, he will believe you in these circumstances, and will agree to keep the horse with you until it wins a race, and will then get rid of it in order to try again with a new purchase.

A good horse — you will find just how rare they are — usually takes very little training. It will act on any going and any course, whether uphill or downhill; it will overcome bad jockeyship, and often mistakes by its trainer.

A bad horse, on the other hand, usually has a mass of

requirements. It won't race on the hard or it can't go on soft ground. It must have the near-equivalent of the champion jockey up before it shows any form. It will not act on a downhill course or will not stay on an uphill one. There is no end to the fads and fancies of the bad horse; yet that, unfortunately, is what you are 75 per cent sure to be training.

The skill needed to cater for all the whims of the bad horse, and possibly to win a race with it when no other trainer could do so, becomes the essential in a trainer's make-up. If he can cope with the bad ones and win with them regularly, it is most likely he will train the good ones equally well.

Noel Murless is a good example of a man who has overcome training bad horses to be at the top of the tree for many years. His first few years as a trainer meant a hard struggle with selling hurdlers and chasers. As far as I can remember, he had nothing of any class for at least 10 years. However, a knowledge of how to cater for the bad is, in my opinion anyway, the reason why he was able to switch (overnight as it were) to training good horses so successfully.

Bad horses do a lot of good for racing, although the poor beasts are never given any credit. They teach trainers and apprentice jockeys; they show owners how to behave as owners should, and above all they give the punter his fun. Without them, racing would be a very boring sport.

In the happy event of the good horse coming along, many worries come with it. The actual training, as I have said, is much the same story, but there is far more worry and mental strain for the trainer.

Whereas your ordinary horse can be kept "simmering" (just as one keeps a pot on the stove in order to bring to the boil at a minute's notice), your good horse must be trained to be at his peak, or boiling point, for a specific occasion. There is a difference between being super-fit for one particular

race, like the Derby or Grand National, and being fit enough
to run whenever required throughout the year. For the super
effort a lot of work is required, and the trainer knows that
once the object is achieved the horse can relax for a while;
whereas his ordinary horse needs to be kept on the racecourse,
and to keep its form, if possible, from March till November.
The trainer therefore trains the ordinary horse on the racecourse, although he would probably not admit it. If he was
to give it the same sort of home preparation as a Classic horse,
he would not last until June before his horse was "over the
top", as we say when the form book shows that the horse has
lost its form.

The mental strain on the trainer of a good horse is far
greater than many people imagine. Most of us say he is jolly
lucky to have such a good horse to train; but it is not all plain
sailing to be in charge of a hot favourite for an important race.
The final week is probably the worst; all the gallops and
preparation have gone according to plan and it is now a
matter of a final sharp bit of work to put the seal on the job.
So often, it is now that things start to go wrong. The horse
leaves his food, which he has not done for two months; or he
seems to be slightly lame and nobody can see any reason for
it, or for some unaccountable reason the horse goes really
badly in his last bit of fast work.

The racing grapevine being what it is, bad news of this
nature, which even you don't know how seriously to take,
will have circulated and a telephone call from the press will
come through. How is your horse? Is it true he has broken
down? Has he got a virus infection? Is it a fact that he went
terribly this morning?

If you only have an ordinary horse, you don't encounter
all this, but as a penalty for training a good horse, you will do.

Although I have never been in the happy position of
training a Classic horse, I have been near enough to know

what happens. If you tell the Press the truth, and say you have not a clue as to what is wrong at this stage, you will appear an incompetent ass. If you say you fear it has a bruised foot, or that it might be getting equine influenza, the horse will go right out of the betting; and when it wins convincingly four days later, you will be dubbed a villain. There really is only one thing to do — make no comment unless you are 100 per cent certain whether the horse is right or wrong. Having done this, you are put down as an unco-operative type, but this is better than being accused of deliberately misleading the public.

A good horse brings all these worries with him and a lot more left unsaid, but they can make you as a trainer, whereas a more care-free life amongst a continual string of bad horses will most likely break you — in the end.

10

Veterinary Help and Shoeing

I hope I shall be forgiven for once more harking back, but in the old days a trainer felt it something of a slur on his ability if the vet's car was seen parked in the yard on numerous occasions throughout the season. His neighbours would nudge each other and say, "I don't know how old Jack would get on without the vet"; and similar caustic comments. However, today the vet is a frequent visitor and trainers have become more and more reliant on his help. No matter how skilled you are, or how knowledgeable you may be about simple jobs, such as stitching a minor wound, giving an injection or rasping a horse's teeth, the safest way to protect yourself is to summon the vet.

I often wonder whether trainers who are also qualified vets carry out their own veterinary work. Or do they feel like the non-qualified and play for safety?

The escalation of bloodstock prices makes us all rush to the telephone; whereas when we knew the horse was not worth a fortune and the vet had 25 miles to come and might not be worth all that when he arrived, we often used to tackle the job ourselves.

In choosing a vet to become your help in all kinds of disasters, I am quite sure you should look for a horseman, as the first qualification. The veterinary profession has improved almost stride for stride with the medical profession; but whereas doctors have only human animals to cope with, vets

have a wide variety. A vet who loves small animals is sometimes scared of a horse, and although he has the knowledge
to do the job, he does not have the necessary bed-side manner.
His first reaction when meeting his patient is one that you and
I would feel if asked to pull out a lion's tooth — a rush for a
strong tranquiliser injection. Fortunately, most training areas
have a good supply of what I call racehorse vets, and it is one
of the new trainer's first jobs to find such a man. Having
found him, stick to him, and pay him too if you can manage it.

Sometimes you may have found the right man but he will
have just taken on a new assistant. The new vet will turn up
when you have an emergency on your hands, and your reaction
will almost certainly be one of complete mistrust — and you
may be right. The assistant may be unused to racehorses, and
your head man will know it. Under these circumstances one
is apt to get a pretty wild diagnosis. One young man, called
in to determine whether a horse had navicular, could not
take his eyes from the horse's fore-legs, which had been fired
two years before and were, although unsightly, perfectly good.
He gave me a long lecture about how horses broke down etc.,
but I could not get him remotely interested in the horse's
feet. I had to get his boss to come out and take an X-ray,
which showed right enough that the trouble was navicular
disease.

On another occasion a horse was lame behind. It again
proved to be the foot, but the new vet spotted what he
was determined to think of as a spavin, and would pay no
attention when told that the bone enlargement on the outside of the hock was due to the horse being kicked at the
start a year ago and had nothing to do with the present
trouble.

Sometimes in your opinion the nearest vet is not the right
man for all your work, but you would still like him for your
cats and dogs, and to do the naming charts, insurance certifi-

cates, soundness certificates for sales, etc. The best policy in this case is to tell him that your regular vet is "so and so" but you would be most grateful if he would agree to do all the other work. Most vets, especially the many Scottish ones in the profession, have the good sense not to turn down money, even if their pride is somewhat injured when they see another firm coming to do the more important jobs.

If you do not make friends with your local vet, you are sure to regret it when an emergency arises. Although, like doctors, a vet will come to anyone's help in an emergency, he will come a lot more quickly and with a better spirit if you have given him all the work you can spare.

I remember once letting down badly one of these local helpful vets, although I was not directly to blame. Our local man had for years done the minor jobs for my father, whereas a vet from Swindon, 25 miles away, did the main work. The local man had over the years established a complete faith in our stable and knowing that we probably knew as much as he did about horses would merely say, "This horse is O.K. — isn't he?", and when told this was so, he would write out a soundness certificate without further ado. We had just received a four-year-old colt from France, and my father rang from London to tell me the horse was now sold (subject to the vet) to go to South America as a stallion, and would I ask the local vet to pass him? "Tell him he is O.K.," father added. I duly showed the vet the horse and told him it was O.K. but a few weeks later a heated correspondence took place between the purchasers and our vet. It transpired that the stallion had only one testicle showing, and even in those days an entire lost a few points for that! I forget how our trusting vet came out of the trouble, but as the stallion proved a great success (firing on one cylinder as it were!), the purchasers no doubt forgave him.

We cannot leave the veterinary side without a word about

anti-equine 'flu precautions, which I wish had never started.

In the days before precautions (either by injection or vaccine) racehorses followed a definite pattern. Yearlings would usually develop colds and then a cough in about October/November, and they in turn often infected the older horses. However, provided the trainer knew his job and relied on all his old-fashioned cold cures, horses would be back to work in 14 to 21 days and would be unlikely to suffer again for another 12 months. In the case of some older horses they seemed to become immune. Once we started "the cure", which everybody, vets included, realised would not deal with all virus infections, we appear to have rocked the boat in no uncertain way. We now have horses coughing at odd times like May and June; and we have a mysterious lack of form, with the only apparent symptoms being a slight trickle in the nostril and a slight thickening in the gullet.

Even if one is strong-minded enough to decline this prevention treatment, the horse's dam and sire have been treated; so whatever good or harm has been done is presumably already in the offspring's blood. Your only hope is to carry on with the same treatment.

Cynics will tell you that the mysterious loss of form caused by an undiagnosed virus is merely a trainer's excuse for his horses running badly, but trainers who have suffered are mostly not only the successful ones but also the most experienced. If they say there is something wrong, I think we should believe them.

After the vet the other most important man to find is a good racing blacksmith.

Farriers, like thatchers and saddlers are becoming fewer. As the carthorse and trap-horse were replaced with the tractor and motorcar, the village blacksmith found himself more in the role of a mender of farm implements than a shoer of horses.

A racing blacksmith is merely one who has the same knowledge as the man who shoes the horses "hot" at the village smithy, but who specializes in making shoes to fit each horse's foot and then takes the shoes to the horse and puts them on "cold". However, thoroughbreds, being highly-strung, awkward creatures, need a horseman to do the job. If this is not the case, it usually means at least one stable lad, who is probably wanted to ride out, must hold the horse.

It was always an eye-opener to me to watch the racecourse blacksmiths at work, in the days when we had all the horses plated on the course. The speed with which Robert Wood and his men could plate about 100 horses in the racecourse yard and never put a nail in the wrong place, was artistry at its highest level. Old shoes would be removed and left outside the box, to be put back on after the race, and a set of aluminium plates of the correct size were attached. The whole job would take about five minutes and if the lad was not there to hold the horse, which he should have been, the blacksmith would either tie up the horse on its wrack chain or, if he knew it well, leave it to nibble away at his shirt whilst he did the job.

It is this familiarity with racehorses (which applies also to the vet) which must be a guide to the man you employ to do this vital job.

When the last war had just started, we were all getting rid of horses out of racing stables in every direction. Some went as remounts, just as they had done 25 years before; some went on a sad trip to the kennels, and others were sold or given away for stud purposes. I rode a nice old mare called Hevusina for 15 miles across Salisbury Plain in order to deliver it in Pewsey, where I had arranged for the village blacksmith to meet me and remove the hind shoes so that I could turn her out in a nearby field. The smithy took one look at poor Hevusina and said, "I ain't touching she, Mister,

but here's the tools and I'll tell 'ee how to take 'em orf.''
This is a case where a craftsman in his own way is asked to
tackle something he is not used to doing. Had I taken a
carthorse or an elderly hunter to him he would have whipped
off the shoes in no time.

If you are based in a racing centre, the shoeing problem is
made simpler because the firm which is already there will
take you on.

However, it is one thing to bustle into the yard and shoe
or plate a horse as quickly as possible; but it is quite another
to study that horse's foot and try to improve it for the future.
The saying "No foot − No 'oss" is a true one. The number of
racehorses who go wrong in their feet is greater today than
ever before unfortunately, I think (but am by no means sure)
that a mare who has gone wrong in her feet can pass on this
defect to her progeny, and a sire too.

If you become successful as a trainer and make a bit of
cash, it is a good investment to employ your own blacksmith
and if possible an apprentice to learn from that craftsman.
This is not a good bargain by way of a profit shown after
you have paid his wages, bought the steel, and installed the
forge; but as regards care of your horse's feet it is worth
every penny.

A skilled man who has 30 to 50 horses to shoe and tend is
much better placed to do the job properly than if he is
chasing around 300 horses in ten or a dozen separate yards.
Your employed farrier is part of the stable team and will get
his few pounds per winner and share the stables victories and
defeats. When you think a horse needs its heels opened or its
toes cut back, you can discuss it with the expert, and it is in
the interests of both of you that the best solution is found.
This is not so easily done with the busy blacksmith, who
really has only contracted to shoe or plate your horse and
often has neither the time nor the inclination to hold an

inquest on how that horse's foot could be made better for the future.

In the past most large racing stables employed their own blacksmiths and would also take on a learner, if the farrier could be persuaded to teach one. In this way the horses of 35 years ago raced far more frequently and for a longer active racing life. We must also bear in mind that there was no such thing as watered racecourses in those days, nor was the ground and going as good and well-prepared as it is today. So it is fair to assume that if our present-day horses appear to be less tough and roadworthy than in the past, it could have a lot to do with the lack of individual attention by an expert in dealing with their feet.

II

A Travelling Head Man

Many trainers have told me that a travelling lad is a luxury which they can do without in these days of cutting costs to a minimum. However, most of these trainers are ones who do not own a horse-box.

It is obviously not economical to have a travelling lad who sits in a public horse-box watching the world go by, and then helps saddle the horse when the trainer is also present.

However, for a trainer starting his new job, I think a good travelling man is as important as a horse-box, providing he can drive the box.

When you start training, you are likely to employ young apprentices or possibly a young girl. Although at this stage it is impossible to leave an entire day's racing for them to carry out alone, the lessons can be learned with the aid of a good, experienced travelling man. From then on, it may be possible to dispense with a travelling lad, but it will only be due to the new intake learning the job, and that will take a few years.

The ideal set-up is to have a good man who can drive the box and also see to the horses. There is so much that can go wrong between leaving the stable and arriving at the racecourse.

To take an example — three young apprentices, or girl grooms for that matter, are sent on a 75-mile journey to the races, driven by a young man in a hired racehorse transport box. The driver has just got the sack from driving sand and gravel lorries, and has taken on this racehorse haulage occupation. He starts as he would with his load of sand and continues in the same way; breaking, cornering etc. are all done with sand, not horses, on his mind. The youngsters' protests on behalf of their racehorses, some perhaps worth £20,000, will go unheeded, and the only time the driver will pay attention is when a pull-in for a cup of tea is suggested.

This sort of journey happens all too frequently, yet how does the trainer know anything about it, unless he has a reliable man to do the journey with his horses? When this is the case, the young driver is soon taught by an experienced travelling head-man that driving racehorses requires a different technique. Also, stops for refreshments will be cut down to a reasonable limit, and when they do happen, the travelling man will see to the very important detail of leaving the horses guarded whilst everyone else goes into the cafe.

My father made Daniel Bee his travelling lad as soon as Danny had finished his five-year apprenticeship, and he was dead right to do so. Danny remained as travelling man for 25 years. He knew his guv'nor's ways and requirements, and was therefore not handicapped as an older man from another stable would have been. In those days the vital question of being able to drive the horse-box did not arise, but there was a great deal of worry and responsibility attached to travelling racehorses all over the country. The railway was the main form of racehorse transport, and looking back on it some forty years later, it is surprising how smoothly and efficiently a large stable of 60 or more horses could travel, also taking along a supply of fodder, paddock clothing, lads' luggage etc.

To travel from Hampshire to race meetings in the north and midlands needed a man with the qualifications of a quarter-master in the services, let alone a stableman. One would land at the station in Birmingham, Nottingham or Glasgow, and then have to arrange the safe passage not only

of one's horses to the racecourse stables, but for three trusses
of hay, two sacks of oats and the lads' possessions as well.
To do this, Danny and his counterparts throughout the country
merely kept a notebook, jotting down what money was spent
and collecting any outstanding cash from their employer
when they got home.

However, that was only the administrative side of the
business. The horses would have to be fed and looked after,
perhaps cantered on the day of the race, or worked fast with
their jockey up. All this was the travelling man's job, and he
would ring his boss at a stated time to report how he was
doing.

If folk say today they can get by without a travelling head-
man, I am sure they could not have done so 40 years ago.
What is more, I don't think that they can do so today with
any lasting degree of success. One cannot be in two places at
once, and therefore the trainer must have someone who is
trustworthy and knows what is required, to carry out his
orders.

The inexperienced apprentice or girl can only do their
best, which is often to look over their shoulder to ask, "What
to do next?" If the new trainer employs a first-class travelling
head-man from the start, he will find that in five years time
his apprentices have learned the job.

It is then a matter of teaching the most promising boy to
drive, which can be a hair-raising experience. I recall allowing
a young man to drive my car from Nottingham races to
Cheshire. We came to a roundabout near Derby, when my
"learner" put his foot on the wrong pedal. We shot across
the road, hit a man on a moped and catapulted him 20 feet
in the air. To my surprise, this innocent chap turned a couple
of somersaults in the air and landed neatly on his feet. It
transpired that he was a trapeze artist in a circus! Thank
goodness he was, because we would have certainly killed

anyone else.

Once one has survived the perilous job of teaching a young person to drive (and remember it was hard enough to teach him to ride four years ago), the time has come to consider what you want him to do at the racecourse, for either a one-day trip or even a stay as long as a week.

The first important thing to get over is that he must always tell the truth regarding the horse's behaviour on the journey, what he looked like after the journey, how much he ate during the night, and how he seemed at exercise next day. All these you must know, especially if you are to advise your owner to have a good bet. If your lad reports all is 100 per cent O.K., when it is not the case, he will have let you down in a big way.

The next items are routine, and provided they become so, the trainer can rest assured that his man will have done them and there will be no need for further checks.

Handing in a declaration form is a job that will be done by your travelling lad about one hour before the first race. He will hold an authority to act, signed by yourself and lodged annually at Weatherbys, to enable him to do it. If you make a point of arriving at the racecourse an hour before the first race, you will find your man in the weighing-room, doing this job, and can learn about your horse's health without a trip to the stable yard.

A point to watch about declaring, is to make sure the jockey is already on the racecourse or is expected by his valet, and that he still intends to ride your horse and has not climbed on to a better one. One is allowed 45 minutes to lodge the form before the time of the race, but provided one has woken up to the fact that the jockey has not arrived, the form can be changed after the allotted time with the Steward's permission.

It is not desirable that a horse should eat anything, especially its straw, for at least two hours before the race. Some trainers make sure of this by putting a muzzle on the horse or by sprinkling strong disinfectant on the litter. This also becomes routine, as does removal of the hay net and water bucket.

After the race it is routine to see that the sheet or "cooler" is covering the sweating horse, and that he is led round to cool off, not to have a bucket of cold water thrown over him and then dragged round a draughty stable yard, stripped naked, as one has often seen. Half a bucket of chilled drinking water is the correct prescription after the race, with more to follow, if required, in an hour's time.

There are endless points of this sort which the trainer will know backwards, but which his apprentice or girl groom will only learn by being told by somebody at the racecourse. They will have learned the stable routine at home, but in the hustle and bustle of a day's racing it is all very different, and it will take many trips and much direction from the man in charge to instil these important details.

The travelling head-lad covering a meeting which you are unable to attend, has an even more responsible job. As well as driving the horse-box 100 miles or more, he will have to look after routine jobs, as well as saddling the horse, meeting the owner, giving the jockey his orders and putting him up, bidding at the auction (if his horse wins a selling race and you have told him to buy it in), appearing before the Stewards as your representative (if he is called upon to do so), deciding on his own initiative if for some good reason the horse should be withdrawn. In effect he represents you in the true sense of the word and holds your licence in his hands. So if you are to train a boy to do the job, he must be the right one and he must be taught by the right man.

Finally, some points about how horses travel may be of interest.

The Levy Board has recently set up its own small racing stable, in order that the veterinary profession can carry out tests and experiments. I suggest it could do some simple tests which I don't suppose trainers have done for themselves. Let us take the case of the Morning Glory, the horse who can beat anything on the gallops, but cannot beat a donkey on a racecourse. All trainers have encountered these infuriating types, and usually they come to the conclusion that the horse is not genuine, and that is that. My experiment would be to load the horse into a horse box, drive him for 100 miles, unload him back on the home gallop and then see if he was still a Morning Glory. I think one may find that it is entirely the travelling which upsets the horse. But it would be interesting to know for certain.

Another simple experiment would be to weigh horses far more frequently than is done now. If, for instance, every training stable and racecourse had a weigh-bridge, it would perhaps, surprise us all to discover how much weight is lost in the journey to the racecourse. I realise trainers who do weigh their horses will know how much the horse has lost in weight by the time it returns home, but that includes the race itself. What I would like to know is how much horses who do not sweat or show any visible signs of bad travelling, lose in weight during a long journey.

Experiments of this nature would help trainers as much as the more advanced anti-equine 'flu research. Even to be able to give a horse a sensible dose of physic as a laxative would be an improvement on our present system, which remains unchanged after 200 years and is about as unsatisfactory now as when it was introduced!

12

Feeding and Stable Management

There is a common saying that "So-and-So is a wonderful feeder", referring to an employee in a stable of horses, whether it is show horses, shire horses, hacks, hunters or even a stud for thoroughbreds.   It means what it says, and that the man in question is a good feeder for the requirements of those particular establishments.

However, a racehorse trainer must, or at least should know exactly what each of his horses eats. In his case a good feeder is the man who does what he is told.

Perhaps the late George Todd was the best example of a trainer who had a long and successful career due to his skill at wielding his own feed bowl.

In the same way that the trainer of a heavyweight boxing champion or the best soccer player in the country watches his charge's diet, so must a successful racehorse trainer.

Your head man, unless he is in fact training the horses for you, cannot possibly know what is required. As the trainer, you know the plans; he does not. Therefore, there must be constant liaison between yourself and your feeder. For instance, if you have just sold a horse to go abroad and have no intention of running it again, it would be stupid, as well as a waste of money, to continue stuffing it with 18lb of oats a day. Also, when you have decided to give a horse a two-month rest, you tell your feeder to "let him down a bit".

These are two very obvious examples, and any trainer will

carry out this drill. Where some may slip up is in keeping a constant watch on each horse's appetite.

A great friend of mine brought me from Spain a china plaque surrounded in wrought iron, entitled "The master's eye fattens the horse". It depicts a very thin man staring point-blank at a very fat horse's belly. Not a pretty picture, but it tells its tale!

If you do leave feeding to your head man, which is the normal routine, a stroll round the yard about two hours after the feed has been given, is well worth the time. A trainer can learn more from these quiet visits to his horses than he will ever pick up from his routine trip at stable time. At approximately 2.30p.m. or 8.00p.m. you are not distracted by other people and there is just your horse to watch in his own private quarters. You can see all sorts of things which you will not see when he is tied up and has been dressed over, perhaps not as well as you would have hoped. Bad habits like crib biting, rubbing the tail on the manger, colts being too colty can all be noted. On top of this there is the important question of eating.

If your head man tells you at 5p.m. that the horse has eaten up the 11a.m. feed, you are pleased, but how much better to know just when he had eaten it all. The trip at 2.30p.m. tells you this. Then there is often the case of the horse which is madly keen for another bowl of oats. If he is due to run and you know he will polish it off in no time, why not go to the feed house and give it to him? The same applies with hay. There is no better reason for having a hay net or rack than to allow you to see just how much has been eaten. When the hay is pitched in on the floor of the horse's box, it becomes impossible to see how much has been eaten and how much has been interwoven in the straw, to be thrown on the muck heap the same day. A horse that is eating well will usually clear his hay net as well as his feed in the manger.

If on your visit the feed has been almost finished but there is still a full hay net, you will leave the box with the knowledge that the horse is O.K. but could be doing better. That knowledge is unlikely to be gained without the touch of individual attention.

As regards the quantity of oats or racehorse cubes to feed, it is impossible to lay down a diet sheet. Each horse has a different appetite and the only useful hints I can give are:—

1.   It is better to feed little and often than big amounts spaced out over long periods.
2.   If a horse is in strong work and ready to run, the more good oats you can get down him the better.
3.   Never give a "breakfast feed" unless it is given at least two hours before the horse does fast work.

In modern times the last point matters most. So often the feed, even if only one bowl of oats, is thrown into a hungry horse's manger at 7am, and the poor blighter is still chewing it when galloping at 8am. If your horses want a breakfast and the head lad does not surface till 6.30am, you should either put back the time of your first lot or get up at 5.30am!

It would be interesting to know how many of the 600 or so stables in the British Isles and Eire have gone over entirely to racehorse cubes, how many do a mixture and how many continue to feed oats in the traditional way.

There are arguments for and against the use of cubes. Possible disadvantages seem to be:

(a)   One is never quite sure of the quality of the oats and other ingredients which go into the cube. Many a scornful head man has said, "Them things are only made from the sweepings out of other people's feed houses!" It seems very unlikely that this should be the case, but it is one of those things one cannot prove. If you are a good judge of oats, you can tell the good from the bad. But how do you judge a cube?

(b)   I found it hard to assess the weight of cubes as given in a feed bowl. We have learned that a normal feed bowl filled level with crushed oats holds approximately 3lb; but does 3lb of cubes equal 3lb of oats? I think we are told so, but trainers and their head men are a cautious lot and therefore are not convinced.

(c)   Hay has always been of very great importance to racehorses, and we were taught that the quality of hay was as important as the quality of oats and bran. With cubes we are told that hay is not necessary, because of the balanced ration already in the cube; and I found that a horse fed entirely on racehorse cubes would not eat as much hay. This to my mind costs the trainer an important yard-stick by which to judge his horse's appetite and general well-being. What is worse is that it deprives the horse of a form of occupational therapy — what is he to do for 22 hours shut in his box and the manger empty?

The advantage of using cubes, and only cubes, is that results seem to be just as good as using oats. If this was not the case, trainers would not use them. Also the cost is less, for although the cubes may be dearer than oats, you will eliminate the cost of two linseed mashes a week, plus a lot of bran, chaff, carrots, grass, treacle etc. If you do away with hay too, it is an even greater saving.

"The proof of the pudding is in the eating"; and if the new trainer finds by asking fellow trainers that they can produce the goods on racehorse cubes alone, he would be silly not to follow suit.

Yet, "It is hard to teach old dogs new tricks", so you will be unlikely to find the older trainers converted. But they could be wrong. Perhaps in time all our old ideas on feeding racehorses will be changed, but one that I feel will never alter, unless a horse's stomach does, is the principle of "little and often".

Vitamins and supplementary feeds will be a headache. "To give or not to give", are questions you will have to answer.

A persuasive salesman — I tried it once but to help the firm, I resigned — will reel off a list of prominent trainers, all highly successful because of using his vitamin additive. No sooner have you settled on this man's product than an entirely different firm approach you with an almost identical treatment. The new salesman has an even longer list of prominent and successful trainers. I found the fairest way out of the quandary was to try each and let the best man win! However, this is impossible because nobody knows how well the horse would have done without either of these undoubtedly good pick-me-ups.

My father's great friend and assistant throughout his 50 years as trainer, Herbert Arnold, had a technique with people selling racehorse tonics. Herbert's approach was: "Let's go and find a horse who needs a bit of help, and if you give me a free course of your stuff and it improves the horse, we will buy from you in a big way." The result of Herbert's pep-talk often used to mean a retreat of the salesman, but if the man had faith in his product and could stand the cost of a sample for a month, we would give it a fair trial on a horse who needed help. In this way we learned if extra vitamins were helping the horse. But to pile a measure into every horse's feed, regardless of his requirement, seems daft to me — and that is no doubt why I was a rotten salesman for a good firm.

The answer is to get the vet to examine a horse who is not doing well, ask him to take a blood test and then ask him what he considers you should give the horse.

The saying "Leave well alone" is a good one. If in your opinion the horse is 100 per cent well, and your trips to the yard have shown you this is so, don't start experimenting; but if he is doing badly, try anything to get him back to peak condition.

Before leaving the question of additives, we should think about the unfortunate trainers whose horses have been found after a race to have a small quantity of a drug in their saliva or urine. As far as I know, in most instances this has been due to giving the horse one of these vitamin additives.

I don't suppose the fact that a horse, weighing half a ton, has consumed the equivalent of a few chocolates or a cup of coffee will make the remotest difference to its form. Nevertheless, the Rules have been broken, and my advice, as a poor salesman but a careful trainer, is to use these products only when necessary; to make quite sure you read the label showing the ingredients, and then to make doubly sure by asking your vet if anything on the label could be detected as a drug.

Old-established firms are by far the safest to buy from, since they cannot afford to risk anything, but whether all horses need their cures, I just don't know.

13

Administration

By now you will have been told countless times what a wonderful life a racehorse trainer leads; and no doubt it is partly because of this that you have taken the plunge.

It *is* a wonderful life and that is why people are prepared to work 16 hours a day at it. One's work is one's hobby, which makes it possible to carry on in a job in which your training account, as produced each year, is highly unlikely to show a profit equal to one of your lad's pay.

The general public sees you dashing to and fro in a decent car, respectably dressed, dining out occasionally with owners (who are footing the bill!) in an expensive restaurant, running up fairly large bills on a credit account at the garage and local shops etc. From all this the evidence is that you are a rich man. Well, it is a good thing to let them keep thinking that way. It is no good looking broke when you *are* broke! "Trainers are such a varied collection of individuals and personalities," was how Mr. Ginnett, a lawyer who acted as secretary for the National Trainers association, once put it to me. How right he was, and for a man who had never encountered the racing world before, what an eye-opener it must have been when he first sat on our committee meetings. No wonder he did not ask for much pay; the entertainment value alone must have made up for it. But, seriously, there can be few trades to compare with racehorse training. There are people in the millionaire bracket doing the job, people who have become rich men by a mixture of skill, hard work and good luck, and a vast majority who have the skill and are capable of hard work, but then — full stop!

In view of this variety of means, it is hard to advise a beginner how he should plan his campaign to deal with the ever-increasing office work. "If you are a rich man," as the song says, it is a matter of employing a good secretary, or even two or three. They will sort out P.A.Y.E., N.H.I., V.A.T., etc.; and one of them at least will man the telephone every morning to deal with withdrawals or declaration by the appointed time. If you are in no position to afford a secretary (and I suspect the new trainer I have in mind is not) you must learn the job from A to Z and either do it yourself, which you will find virtually impossible during peak racing times, or teach your wife, children or another voluntary helper.

Every new scheme thought up to help the stay-at-home punter, man-in-the-street, buyer of racing papers, or whoever, has thrown more work on to two sets of shoulders: the trainer's and Weatherbys'. Overnight declarations were brought in to help the punter, but one has to wonder if they have helped him half as much as they have hindered everyone else! In the days before this bright idea, liaison between press and trainers produced a 98 per cent correct result in the morning papers. We now have the same result, but a trainer will usually be fined £25 for not running his horse when he knows full well it is in everybody's interest not to run.

Overnight declaration of blinkers, we were told, was vital and essential for the punter; but I have found that the best bet of the year is to lay every horse who wears blinkers for the first time out. This is a really safe bet!

The next "essential" will be to declare jockeys overnight — and I wonder how much good that will do for the punter? Admiral Rous (at least I think it was him) decided that only 7lb separated the worst apprentice from the best jockey; so what gain will there be if the punter knows overnight that Lester is riding instead of Willie?

Nobody likes to read in the Racing Calendar that they have been fined and to avoid this you will have to run the gauntlet. Every day you must think about which horses must be left in or withdrawn, which have blinkers declared, and no doubt some time in the future, which jockey is to ride. All this will cost you a call to the Weatherbys' nerve centre at Wellingborough before 11am, and if you fail to get through, you just grin and bear the fine! No good-doer, like the admirable Jack Logan of the *Sporting Life*, will suggest that your calls to Weatherbys should be paid for, or for that matter that you should receive the Racing Calendar free of charge, or that your postage for the entries should be met. That is because you are assumed to be a rich man — and so far the good-doers have only just got around to making sure you will have to pay your staff about twice what you receive for working double their hours! This sounds rather bitter but as I have stressed before, I am not trying to put you off, but merely attempting as best I can to put you right.

Obviously when you reach the stage of 30 horses, all fully paid for, it is time to consider whether you can afford a secretary. There will be many days when you are away or busy with an owner watching his horses at work, so you can't possibly be doing this expensive and aggravating chore on the telephone at 10am. You may have trained your wife or child; you may not have either to train, or they may not even be trainable. In any case, you will find that as your staff increases the paying of the lads is going to be a headache. Every week the money must be drawn from the bank and your staff paid correctly; and N.H.I. stamps must be collected from the Post Office and put on the men's cards. Even for a ten-horse stable, you must think in terms of an outlay of approximately £80 a week in this direction.

Reverting to the secretary, I am speaking from my own experience and inability to deal with any of that P.A.Y.E., V.A.T. etc. I would have found it essential to have somebody who came in once a week and did the job, but for the fact that firstly my landlord and secondly my wife did it for me. However, if you are to steer clear of the law, you must have expert help from the start on the wages side. Many well-meaning trainers have got into trouble in various ways, such as by not disclosing winner money, travelling money, and bonuses paid to their lads. Worse still, the man who is going badly and misses a few weeks of stamping N.H.I. cards can find himself in serious trouble. A trainer friend of mine left it all to "The Major", his new-found help and secretary; but what the trainer did not know at the time was that the £50 a week designed for the lads' stamps was invested by The Major at the local betting shop! At least £500 had gone astray before the trainer found out what was going on.

If you are lucky to find a man who serves other trainers, he will draw the money, pay the men, and keep that side of the job straight in about one hour's work per week. The other part of the paper work you will have to do as best you can.

Even when you can afford a secretary, most of the office work must be decided by you, even if the typing and copying is carried out by someone else. Making of entries, withdrawal of horses overnight, acceptance at the four-day stage, and writing or telephoning owners must all come from the trainer's brain, though the task itself may be done by the secretary.

The whole question of administration in a racing stable is so much dependent on the capital available. It is not simply a matter of being able or unable to afford a secretary, but how and when to buy fodder which really counts in the long run. If you can buy a year's supply of oats and hay in October and pay on the nail, you are in a very favourable position. It means you should not use either until after Christmas if they are harvested in the current year, but provided you have suitable storage, you will be buying at the right time and will save a lot of money.

In the old days trainers were far more inclined to "shop around" than they are today. Instead of ringing the local hay and corn merchant to order another load of clover mixture hay, without even counting the cost, they rode by with their string and watched the farmer's efforts. If the trainer saw that it was a decent bit of hay and well made, he would then approach him to buy the stack. In this way he knew what he was buying, and if the cost of getting it tied out in those old-fashioned trusses and the transport was not too dear, he was far more likely to have first-class hay at the right price than he is today. This can still be done if you have the time and energy. The hay will be baled and not stacked loose, which is a pity from the horse's point of view, but in most training areas it is still there waiting to be bought if only you make the effort.

Once the dealer does this job for you, he quite understandably charges his fees, and you are thus paying more cash, although the farmer has only received what you would have bid him.

I know this sounds simple in these hectic times, but when you start up, you have this opportunity to shop around. If you buy good stuff and cut out the dealer, you will, at least for the first year, have obtained the best of the fodder bargain and will have learned a lot about what is required at the same time.

When I started up in Cheshire, I tried out these ideas. I had seen a nearby farmer making some very nice mixture hay, and when he had it safely gathered, I dropped in to see him. I bid him a fair price and I think he was keen to sell, but at the time I did not understand the routine of a farming deal north of the Trent. The farmer came out with what I learned was a standard reply to my inquiry of "Will you sell your hay?" by saying, "I'm not fussed." I merely told him if he was that dis-interested, I would look elsewhere! I did not then know the form, and next day the same farmer, who was very anti-racing, drove his tractor flat out at my horses and put us all in the ditch! The police brought a case against him and he was fined a few pounds, but naturally all further hay dealings were out. If only I had known enough to translate, "I am not fussed" into, "I am keen to sell", I might have had a good supply on the doorstep for the next ten years.

Oats are in much the same category as hay from the buying angle. However, in both cases, especially if you buy through a dealer, listen to the market prices and don't go rushing to give £40 a ton when the stuff is sold at £20 per ton every day in the market. Likewise, if you are convinced that Australian or Canadian oats are better than ours and that you should pay £10 per ton extra for them, I suggest you have them analysed and weigh them when crushed. In this way you will know whether the extra money is worth investing.

Straw is a subject about which I have strong views, and therefore I may be rather biased, but it is my belief that straw for racehorses' bedding should be abolished and something more hygenic, more comfortable, and safer substituted. The straw which you will buy bears no comparison with the old-fashioned long wheat straw. You will often get some very short and mouldy stuff which for weeks has been standing in the field. If anything is likely to produce the mysterious viruses of which we hear so much, it is bad straw. Time will decide, but it seems a safe bet that if farmers prefer to burn the stubbles instead of baling the straw, there will not be any more wheat straw suitable for bedding down horses or thatching houses. Then we must think again, and perhaps a fitted carpet of strong rubber would be more useful.

If this ever came about, the mucking out process would be made far easier, injuries caused by a brick or concrete floor avoided, and infection from dust minimised.

14

Within the Law

When a trainer receives his licence, he also receives a booklet entitled "Rules of Racing and Instructions by the Stewards of the Jockey Club". Like all books of rules, it makes for rather dull reading and I doubt that many trainers do more than glance at it, let alone learn and study the individual rules.

In fact, rather in the way that motorists seem to get by without knowing the Highway Code by heart, trainers manage by knowing only the rules that affect them in their jobs.

Fortunately, if there is a change, it is always well publicised, so trainers seldom delve into the book of rules.

However, to keep within the law, the more a new trainer studies the book of rules the better.

Once he has grasped the Rules which concern him, he is well advised to let his apprentices and lads have the previous year's copy.

It always seems wrong to me that stable lads are seldom given the chance to become acquainted with the Rules of Racing, and many of them become trainers and travelling head-men still not having seen the rules of their profession.

Taking, for example, the putting up of your apprentice for his first ride, there are plenty of rules to be broken if the new trainer has not done his homework. A skull cap must be provided. The boy must ask permission at the start to have his girths checked. The trainer or his representative must be present at both the weighing-out and weighing-in stages. The boy must be conversant with the course, i.e. must have walked it. If the ride is for another trainer, the booking must have been made by the boy's master and not by the boy himself.

These are a few which spring to mind, but there are further things for which you will be held responsible, although they are not all rules. If there is any form of inquiry by the Stewards, you or your authorised agent must be available to appear before the Stewards with your apprentice. If he wins the race or is placed, and in his excitement fails to weigh in, it is you, not the boy, who carries the can.

The simple rule that says "No trainer shall employ any person who has previously been in a training stable without referring to his last employer and receiving a satisfactory reply in writing" is possibly the most abused rule in the book.

With racing labour in such short supply, and I am afraid to say as bad as it is today, trainers are so desperate to find lads that there is seldom a written reference, and if they are written a great many could not be termed satisfactory.

Take the case of a trainer trying his best to keep up a standard of stable management, who will order a lad to get the sweat marks out, or wash out a horse's feet and the lad merely says, "Right, if you want it that way, I'm off." The trainer, who may be one of the do-it-yourself types and has to do the lad's three horses, is in no mood to write a glowing testimonial. However, the lad is O.K. because he knows that a trainer nearby is desperate, and will take him on . . . and so it goes. You must give some sort of reference, but whereas a few years ago a bad reference would stop a racing lad from getting a job, today it seems to make little difference.

"To keep within the law", as I have put it, apart from obeying these rules, is mainly a matter of how you run your horses. We read a lot about the number of non-triers, but after what seems a very long time watching and participating in racing, I agree with whoever said that there are less non-triers now than ever before.

The trouble is that to spot a genuine non-trier needs far more skill than the average punter, or the average Stewards' secretary for that matter, possesses. So much depends on how the horse needs to be ridden.

I trained a horse which, by trial and much error, I found could only win if he was taken to the back of the field from the start. This used to lead to terrible rows and inquests when his joint-owners, plus all their knowledgeable friends, joined the horse, jockey and myself after a defeat. If it was a slowly-run race, our horse would be taking his usual "nap" about 20 lengths behind the leaders at the halfway stage in a 1½-mile race. As the pace increased, the horse would be left with too much to do and his long run over the final two furlongs would end in a narrow defeat. Disgruntled punters would swear the horse was not trying, and the equally disgruntled owners would be convinced that if he had taken closer order, he would have won. The fact remained that this particular horse was no good unless ridden in this way. He won plenty of races when allowed to do it his way, and never won when asked to take an interest early in the race. I quote this as one sort of horse who can get you into trouble.

Another type is the horse who will not run on under the whip. You know this and your jockey knows it, but when you get beaten by a head, everyone else seems to know that if the jockey had not taken things so easily the horse would have won. In both examples your horse will be deemed by most people to be a non-trier.

Fortunately, the Stewards and their secretaries are not so dumb as one is led to believe. For any crime there is usually a motive, and I think, or at least I hope, that their inquiries into non-triers are based more on the motive than on what they fear they may have seen. If, for instance, your horse, who has run one of these "suspicious" races starting at 20/1, is backed down to favourite next time out ten days later and wins in a canter, you will need to have all your excuses ready to meet the cold eyes behind the table in the Stewards' room.

"You've got to pick a pocket or two" is a quote from the musical world which may be rather too suggestive; but there will come a time, especially when trying to win a good handicap, when the trainer must in some way try to beat the handicapper.

Before the computer-assisted system of handicapping, one could go up to a handicapper and ask him, "How in the world did you manage to give this poor horse so much weight?" This was fun at the time, but to play the game fairly, one did it prior to the race, and then very often saw one's poor over-burdened nag romp home — unbacked — and so the handi-capper had the last laugh.

How you deal with a computer I have no idea, but if you are to beat it, an occasional "well-within-the-law scheme" will have to take place. Some horses handicap themselves, as my father used to put it, by which he meant that a horse will strike form regularly at a certain time of year. We say, for instance, that September/October is a filly's best racing time. There are, however, horses of either sex which come to their best by August, and the trainer need only run this type in handicaps from March till July (in each race trying for its life) to get it down in the handicap. It then strikes form in August and wins three races on the trot. It will be interesting to see how the computer catches one of these.

The spring horse, perhaps a Lincoln Handicap candidate, can also run down the course all year after his race but will return with a lower weight and at the peak of condition the following spring.

In these instances no rules are broken: it is the horse who has obligingly conformed.

There are other occasions when, if the horse is not so obliging as to stop himself in order to get his handicap down, he has to be assisted.

Many years ago Herbert Smyth (known as Nat) referred to a jockey of his as "The Undertaker". When, in my youthful ignorance, I asked why, Herbert said: "Because he would undertake to stop anything." No doubt in those days a good loyal "Undertaker" in the yard was a god-send, but there are none left today! No trainer hoping to keep his licence tells a jockey to stop his horse. In the case of a trainer who has only taken on the jockey for a spare ride, for instance, the jockey would naturally tell all his friends and punters how he had pulled the horse; and where would you be next time out when you wanted a bet at a long price?

My father was always described as very shrewd by the Press, which really meant he was not above "stopping" one for a coup. This indeed was the case, but as he trained more winners than anyone else, I doubt that a great number of would-be winners were stopped.

There is a method in good trainers producing a horse at its best on the day when wanted, which is an art and not a form of deceit.

If the horse is intended to win a good handicap in June, his previous races are stepping-stones. Possibly the trainer will put the horse in races slightly out of its distance, running a six-furlong horse over a mile, or a miler over a sprint distance. He may know that the horse will act far better in blinkers, but will keep them in reserve for the big day. He may run the horse in very poor company, which makes victory, especially a narrow one, hard for the handicapper to assess. He may put up an apprentice from his own stable in the knowledge that the horse needs a better jockey. In this way he gives the boy much-needed practice, and since the horse is carrying 7lb less for the apprentice allowance, it will help when the handicap comes out.

All are legitimate forms of racing tactics, and it would be hard for a trainer to complete his career without occasionally adopting them.

It is the orders given to a jockey which decide whether you stay within the law. Personally, I do not believe that any good trainer ever tells the jockey to pull a horse. If he does, he is not only a knave, but a fool.

The orders for what we will call an unfancied runner are more likely to be on these lines: "Win of course if you can, but he has been a bit off colour and may need the race. Don't knock him about if he tires." The good trainer knows near enough how fit is the horse and that these orders are 99 per cent sure to guarantee the horse a nice easy race. Furthermore, if by chance both himself and the jockey are interviewed separately by the Stewards for not trying, they can come out with the same tale.

The unwise trainer who asks a jockey point blank to stop a horse, especially one that would have been an easy winner, not only jeopordises his own career but also that of his jockey.

Since the camera patrol came into force, there can have been few instances of this blatant infringement of the Rules. It was one thing for a jockey to lose a race a mile from the stands, but it is quite another to do it when under the microscope all the way.

15

Entries, Fines and Frustrations

"Little ships should stay near the shore" was one slogan on which I was brought up. Another well-known amongst trainers is, "Keep yourself in the best company and your horses in the worst." "Little fish are sweet" is a third maxim; but they all add up to — "Don't overestimate your horse's ability."

It does so much good to a horse to win a race and so much harm to be over-faced.

I think perhaps we sometimes do not put ourselves and our reactions into a racehorse's life as much as we should. If any of us is continuously beaten at running, billiards, tennis or any other game one cares to mention, we simply become what is called a "good loser". Racehorses have a large majority of "good losers" amongst their 10,000 population, and I think perhaps many of them have reached this comfortable state by being entered for races which they have no earthly chance of winning, no matter how hard they try.

Horses are not intelligent, but they do "register" enough to know that they like to be able to run faster than their neighbour, just as small children do. When they find they are outpaced from the start and then hit a few times at the finish by an over-keen rider, they lose confidence, and from then on are content to "fall in behind".

The most important job of the week for a trainer is to tackle the entry sheet. The man who can place his horses well is almost certain to do better than the man who cannot do this important job.

With a full week's work and perhaps as much as 1,000 miles driving to and from the races, the entry sheet becomes rather a rushed job on Sunday, which is really the only day when one can get down to it. Sunday, the day of rest, is usually far removed from its Christian ideal in a trainer's life. Owners like to come to see you and their horses on a Sunday. Jockeys are free to ride work, and if you have an important gallop to do for a race in the near future, it will often take place on Sunday. Some of your lads, quite understandably, will want the day off, and the ones who are left, will expect a very easy day.

In fact, if the clergy complain of lack of attendance at their morning service, trainers have a better alibi than anyone else!

There are many different methods of entering horses. One can grab the form and fill in every horse in the yard for whichever race it is qualified. This hit-and-miss system appears to be popular these days, when as many as 12 horses are entered by the same trainer for the same race. But, to be fair, we must consider the circumstances before we criticise this apparent over-spending. Let us suppose the trainer has 15 maiden three-year-olds and at least 30 two-year-olds to enter. If he becomes too selective in his entries, it is doubtful whether he would ever get half of them entered at all. The races are only there once and if you miss the chance too often you find you have not got the horse entered when it is "raring to go".

Likewise, I have seen trainers criticised for entering horses which are not qualified. This, of course, happens and can be the result of carelessness; but when we see about ten horses N.Q. for a particular race, it is more likely to be because of a change in the condition of the race. The trainer who for years has entered for and often won a race called the Blank

Selling Plate, for 3-year-olds to be run over 6 furlongs at a certain course, is apt to take for granted that the conditions will remain as they have been for the last 25 years. A new Clerk of the Course, however, will have changed the condition of the Blank Selling Plate stipulating that it is now to be run for 2-year-olds — hence the trainer's mistake. We know he is wrong, but had the name of the race been altered when the conditions were changed, it would have stopped trainers from making fools of themselves in their Sunday rush.

There are many such pitfalls facing the trainer. For instance, I could not believe my eyes when Pontefract turned their Upton Selling Plate, over 1¼-miles for three and four-year-olds, into a two-year-old race of the same distance. In common with many other trainers I took it for a misprint and entered a four-year-old! However, Pontefract stuck to their guns (misprint or not) and ever since have had the dubious honour of racing two-year-olds over 1¼ miles.

Before we had a four-day acceptance, trainers tackled their entries in a rather more businesslike fashion. They asked themselves the vital question, "Does the horse need a race?" before they entered. Now it has become a matter of, "If it is qualified, let's enter it and see what the four-day acceptance looks like." This, of course, only applies to what we term "run of the mill" horses. To a certain extent the high-class ones will have a programme laid down, and it is a fact that to enter a good horse is a far easier task than to "shop around" in order to pick up a small winning stake with a moderate one.

Trainers who are obviously skilled at making entries, or at what is termed placing their horses well, are usually those with a lot of experience, which helps them pick the right race.

It is not simply coincidence when a trainer wins the same race year after year, with a different horse each time;

it is because he knows just what is needed for the job. A punter would be well advised to spot trainers who "farm" certain races and to follow them whenever they have entries.

Having touched on the business of entering horses, it is time to look at what we once knew as the forfeit stage.

Since the advent of four-day acceptance, there is a definite incentive for the trainer to stay in races, perhaps at two or three meetings, with the same horse. There is method in this apparent madness, and the owner is quite prepared to outlay a few pounds in order to win a race.

Having left your horse in at, say, Ayr, Doncaster and Wolverhampton, you have three full days to decide which race to go for. There are many factors to consider, the most likely ones being:

(a) Which race is going to be the easiest?
(b) Which course will be most likely to provide the going to suit the horse?
(c) Which race is most likely to allow engaging the jockey you have in mind?
(d) Which race suits the owner?

During the three clear days you find the answers, or at least you try to do so. You may also, by a few shrewd inquiries, find out which race your main "dangers" are going for. This can often be done whilst engaging a jockey. You ring the jockey and say, "Can you ride Jackpot in the 3.30 at Ayr?", and he says, "Very sorry, I ride So and So in that race." You leave the phone knowing your "danger" is definitely running at Ayr, and furthermore has the jockey you particularly wanted in the saddle. This information probably rules out Ayr. You then try again with other jockeys and possibly the local Press man (whom I have always found to be the greatest help, provided I co-operated). Finally, after spending about £2 in telephone calls, you have the information necessary to decide in which of the three races you will run.

The next important job is to declare the horse for the race by 11am on the day before the event.

Failure to run is often accompanied by a fine. The most common fine is imposed when you have travelled the horse, your staff and yourself some 200 miles, only to find that the going, in your opinion, is not suitable for that particular horse.

I have never been one to say: "The Jockey Club should — the Jockey Club must, etc. etc." Not that I am scared of them; I merely respect their position and admire how well for centuries (if left to their own devices) they have managed British racing.

However, I don't think many trainers agree with the existing system of being fined for not running. The whole aspect of the business is wrong and we all know it. Stewards, owners, trainers and jockeys all know that if a horse is forced to run on going which is not suitable, it is in *nobody's* interest for that horse to run.

The going or state of the ground is the crux of the matter. How is it determined? The Clerk of the Course, who is responsible for the description, is biased to the extent that he obviously wants runners, but has he the necessary know-ledge to know just what the going is to be at, say, 3.30pm on the day?

To assess the state of the going on a racecourse, you have to imagine you are riding on it. To prod a tentative umbrella into the grass at 5pm the day before can give no clue at all, even if a Fred Archer or Sir Gordon Richards wielded the umbrella. Unfortunately for trainers, it is this touch of the amateur, done a few hours before their race, which determines the state of the going as published and often displayed on the number board.

When you have travelled 200 miles, intending to run a horse with bad joints who cannot race on the firm, and decide in your own mind, he will be 75 per cent certain to break down if he did run, you will walk the course and try as hard as you can to convince yourself that the going is as good as described.

However, when you stamp your foot or (if young and active) jump six inches and land on your heels, your teeth are loosened or the odd molar, who has slept quietly for a year, is now aching. The next step is to find the Clerk of the Course and ask permission to withdraw your horse. The final step is an interview with the Stewards, who will hear you with sympathy but point out that the going is officially described as good, and therefore you will be fined £25 for not running.

There are few things in racing I consider unjust, but this is one of them. Furthermore, I feel that as these £25 fines increase in number, instead of being swallowed up with all the other fines to go towards Racing's Administrative Fund, they should be put aside to help directly the owners and trainers who have paid them.

To be fined when you are in the wrong is one thing; to be fined when you are in the right and only protecting your horse is quite another.

Instead of saying, "The Stewards must, etc.", I will say, "That no doubt the stewards *will* see that for many years there has been a miscarriage of justice, and from henceforth a new system will be put into operation and the odd million taken from innocent trainers and owners will be refunded!" If this ever happens — which I am afraid even my faith cannot hope for — what a number of worthy causes could benefit from all that fine money.

Financing trainers to keep a horse to teach their boys; free postage of entries and racing calendar; free phone calls etc.: they would all help the trainers' cares if only the ruling body sees the light.

16

Private Gallops

Although it is more likely you will rent property which has been a racing stable for many years, in which case there will be gallops in the vicinity, you may find you have to start from scratch with your gallops.

There still remain many old ancestral homes with large stable yards and parkland, no longer used in the way intended a hundred years ago when they were built and laid out. The large mansion may be a school or institution; the park may be let to a local farmer for grazing, and the stables are sometimes left to rot. It is amazing how well-built and sound many of these stables are, in spite of years of inactivity. Some stable blocks, attached to large country houses, are better than many racing stables regarding lads' accommodation, tack rooms and loose boxes.

The answer for this is fairly obvious. Often a rich landlord of the last century, whose main occupations were hunting and racing, was inclined first to have built an ideal place for his hunting activities, and then in another part of the country a training establishment for his racehorses and trainer. If the money still held out, a stud would be built elsewhere.

This ancestral-home type of stables is ideal for the new trainer, and I think it well worth his while looking for fresh territory of this sort, rather than thinking that in order to train well he must go to a recognised area or to a stable which has been vacated by another trainer.

Once you have found the right place, with 30 good loose boxes, a head man's house, good lads' accommodation and somewhere for yourself, you can make sure the ground is suitable for your gallops. Surprisingly enough, one does not need a vast acreage, and in my opinion the two essentials are four furlongs plus a pulling up space of straight and level going, and a mile and a quarter circuit. Without the possibility of these, you had better look elsewhere. Naturally, a longer straight and a longer circuit are better, but it is surprising of how small an acreage these two essentials consist.

An acre being 22 yards by 220 yards, your five-furlong gallop is five acres and your mile and a quarter circuit is ten. The more land is available the better, provided it includes the two essentials.

Parkland is often most suitable for training horses. The turf has usually remained undisturbed by the plough for many years, and even if cattle and sheep share it with the horses, it is a risk worth taking. If the park in question is 75 acres and you are to rent the land, it will be a costly business, and in order to keep down the grass and to try to pay the rent you will find it necessary to stock it with beasts or sheep anyway. And if the landlord is already being paid a fair rent by the farmer, it is highly probable that if permission is granted to exercise your horses in the park, the charge will be no more than a nominal one. Cattle and sheep who share gallops have bad habits other than occasionally getting in the way. They often make paths, usually to the water trough, and if these hard-worn tracks cross your gallop, or worse still go straight down it, their nuisance value will outweigh the good they do.

Cattle, from the smallest calf to oldest dairy cow, seem to take a fiendish delight in knocking down or pulling to pieces anything newly erected on what they consider their property. Schooling fences and hurdles, a starting gate or starting stalls will all take a caning. However, one knows what to expect and it is possible to either use an electric fence or barbed wire which has to be taken down and put back after schooling.

My father used to employ a schoolboy in the summer holidays to keep the cows away from fences which he had made up in late August. The boy, having decided that the cows were peacefully grazing well away from the jumps, decided to take a nap behind one of the fences and awoke to find three horses abreast, jumping his fence, and him too.

Because of its age this parkland turf usually has its advantages for a gallop, since there will be some "spring" in it during dry weather and "toughness" in wet. The older is a pasture the stronger and more closely-knit become the roots, and small fibrous weeds and moss all tend to form a carpet, which is not the case on any newly-sown field.

The other important factor to be considered when selecting ground for gallops is soil. Heavy land such as clay is not much good, even if it is under old turf. In a dry spell it will "bake" and in wet weather the horses' feet will sink in to the depth of three or four inches. A light loam soil, such as chalk produces, or a sandy soil are best. In these cases you get a certain amount of "give" in hard-going periods, and although a horse will cut it up as he gallops in the wet, he does less harm to himself and to your gallop than he would by sinking a hole with each foot as it hits the ground.

If you have rights to use all the park, which is highly probable if you are allowed in at all, you can concentrate on keeping your straight and circuit in the best condition, saving them for fast work only. There is no doubt that the best way to keep a gallop in perfect condition is not to use it!

It is vital to return the gallop to its state of perfection when you use it. The only way to do this is to replace the divots as the golfers say, or tread in the tracks, as racing folk put it. It is a boring job to walk around a mile and a quarter circuit, putting back every piece of misplaced turf; but it is not hard work, nor does it take as long as many people think. One hour is ample time. You need only a good pair of feet and a small four-pronged fork, like the border fork designed for lady gardeners. You then scrape the loose turf back into position with the fork and put your foot on it. In the event of a hoof-print being "counter-sunk", you ease the fork underneath to raise the centre of the print and again tread on it to level the ground. Short cuts, like pulling the roller or chain harrows over the tracks, will not achieve the best results. On hard going, when the horses' foot-prints can barely be seen, the chain harrow is a help, but in soft or even good going you will pull the turf away from its natural resting place.

The roller is a lethal weapon if used at the wrong time. If you pull the roller over holes in the ground, you not only fail to close the hole with the misplaced turf but you also flatten the sides of the hole, leaving a series of "flower-pot" type holes which fill with rainwater and thus rot the surrounding turf. The time to use a roller — a cambridge, with rims on it, is best — is from October to March, preferably when you are not going to use the gallop. In this way you get rid of the lumps and bumps and leave a level surface for the following summer. If, however, you have a really good covering of grass on the gallop and wish to use it all winter, use the roller two days before you gallop the horses and then get your fork and feet working to put back the tracks.

To roll the ground in April and through the summer is wrong. It works all right on tennis courts and croquet lawns, but not on gallops. The effect of rolling after the wet spell in April will look good at the time, but what you will do is close all the "pores", and after a spell of dry, sunny weather, your gallop will become more suitable for an airport runway than an area on which to try the two-year-olds.

Chain harrows are far less dangerous and the time to use them is when you have put the roller away. March, April and May, when your new grass is coming, is the time to pull out all the old dead grass and allow the new to come through.

The other tool needed is a mower. Since the gang mower came into use, racecourses and gallops have improved out of all knowledge. Continual cutting and scattering of the clippings thickens the carpet. We all do it on our lawns, yet seldom stop to ask ourselves why the going on the tennis lawn is so much better than on the gallops.

I once employed an enthusiastic Spaniard, who used to set off pushing a 16-inch rotary motor-mower (which was all I had) on a marathon trip around a mile and a half gallop. The results were good and a derelict gallop became a first-class one in three months, but the Spaniard got crafty and built himself a seat on the mower, which proved too much for the engine. I should have put a pair of blinkers on him and made him keep walking!

There are many further improvements which can be made as regards fertilising. However, if as in the case stated, sheep and cattle share the gallop, I am not sure that putting down peat-moss or farmyard manure is worth it. Already you will have found that from the efforts of the roller, harrows, and cutter your bit of turf is greener and more desirable than the rest of the park. Therefore, the sheep and cattle will spend all their time on it and further encouragement will make matters worse. However, if sheep and cattle are not involved, I am a firm believer in peat-moss. It is easy to stand one or two horses on peat instead of straw and to use this litter straight from the box on to the gallop. The fibrous nature of peat helps to keep the jar out of the ground, and the manure effect produces growth.

If cattle and sheep are not involved, a lot can be done by fertilising, provided one carries out the basic principles of track treading, rolling, harrowing and cutting with a rotary

cutter. There is, however, always a danger in "jazzing up"
this old turf. You must always remember it is not what it
looks like, but how it "feels" to the horse galloping on it
which is important. The more manure and treatment you
give the gallop the greener and better it will look, but might
you may not have got rid of those old creeping weeds and moss
which made the going so nice?

A further word about private gallops concerns the use of
a plough or sand gallop.

During the summer, when gallops and racecourses are
often extremely hard, it is possible to keep racing a horse,
provided he is not continually asked to canter, let alone
gallop, on hard going at home. This is where plough of some
sort is essential. The months involved are May to August,
but how this will work in our ancestral park set-up I have no
idea. All that is required is approximately a five-yard breadth
of plough to extend for four to five furlongs, and if this can
be in the form of a circuit so much the better. If it is not
possible to disturb the ancient turf, a nearby farmer may
allow use of a head-land around one of his corn fields.

The plough gallop is not only an essential, but it also
presents few problems. If the land is very stony, you must
clear the larger stones; but apart from that, attention remains
a simple matter of pulling a set of spike or disc harrows over
it twice a week.

All these ideas on making and maintaining one's own
private gallop may sound like hard work and expense to a
new trainer, but this is not the case. A second-hand Land
Rover, which need not be licensed if kept on the gallops, a
set of chain harrows, a set of spike harrows, a cambridge
roller and a mower is the total outlay. Even today £200
would meet this cost, and it is good for a few years. If you
can't do the work yourself, about four hours labour a week
will be enough, and if that is directed properly, the gallops

could be just as good as in a training area.

It seems, therefore, there is a very good case for the man who has his own private yard and gallops. He can charge owners enough to cover expenses, save his owners a set charge (as in an established area) and give himself a lot of interest. What is most important, his horses will benefit considerably by the changes and improvements made by the trainer.

17

Schooling a Hurdler

Racehorse trainers do not take holidays in their climb up the ladder to success. The time to think about a holiday is when you have made enough to be able to afford one! These words may sound hard, but if anyone cares to do a tour of the 600 trainers he will find that only about 25 per cent have a holiday at all, and only about five per cent leave this country.

As we mentioned earlier, a trainer's work is also his hobby. If the same man took a job in a factory, doing a monotonous task, he would put in far less hours of work but would definitely need a holiday. The trainer who, starting with ten horses, has after two years collected 30 and filled his yard, is unlikely to pack up with his wife and children and move out to the West Indies for the winter. More likely, having done his best with the Flat horses and being in possession of a horse-box, his next idea is to apply for a jumping licence.

Although competition over the jumps is very strong, there always seems to be a way to gain a few easy victories with one's Flat horses, and that can best be done from September to December, and again in April and May. A good trainer will do this without spoiling the horse for the Flat, and he may also improve the horse.

Towards the end of your second year as a trainer you may have some three-year-olds who stay 1¼ miles or perhaps only seven furlongs, and are built to jump and to carry 11st. instead of 8st. It is for these animals that taking out a jumping licence is worthwhile.

For some strange reason, a Flat-race trainer applying for a jump licence in July does not seem to encounter the same official opposition as might a jump trainer who applies for a Flat licence in January, yet it is said there are far too many jumpers. Let us skip this debate and assume you have been granted a licence to run your horses from the start of the jumping season in August.

A lot must have been written about schooling racehorses, but if so, I have never read it. Therefore, I feel free to pass on my own ideas, for what they are worth.

A first principle, which is often neglected, is to provide the horse with something solid to start with. A tree trunk, even if only two-feet high, is worth more than a flimsy, broken-down three-foot hurdle. Although it is against anything I was taught, I think that in these days of inadequate riders, and with the cost of jumps to be considered, a loose school is advisable. If one creates a straight channel 50 yards long (preferably against a hedge or wall to save labour), making sure the barriers at the ends and sides are adequate, one can place two small, solid jumps and allow the horse to learn its own way by letting him loose and encouraging him to jump.

As I have said, I do not believe in this method for schooling racehorses, because the man on the horse must be the pilot, and if from the start the horse is given confidence by its rider to take off when told to do so, the lesson, once learned from the right man, will stand the horse in good stead all its life. But sometimes we have to "cut the cloth to suit the coat".

To revert to the solid jump for the beginner, this is essential, whether in a schooling lane or out in the open. All horsemen schooling jumpers realise that unless the horse has learned the most important elementary lesson, to pick up its feet, it will go on for years knocking down any obstacle which is soft enough to be knocked down.

It is a fallacy that the best hurdlers hit every hurdle, or that the best steeplechasers hit every fence. The horse which has learned to stand back, clear the obstacle and land far out on the other side will gain lengths on the rival who hits every jump. What is more, the good jumper not only gains ground but does not take so much out of himself.

If you do not settle for the loose-school plan, make two small solid hurdles and stuff them with gorse. It is a mistake to think that "the poor horse will prick its legs and you are being cruel." You will be far more cruel if you allow the horse to think he can knock down everything without consequence, in which case your horse will charge the first obstacle it meets on a racecourse and possibly break its neck or the jockey's.

Once you have got the horse jumping alongside a more experienced horse over the two hurdles, it is time to tackle two or three flights equivalent to racecourse hurdles. These hurdles, made of ash-wood, are costly but if you look after them, storing them during the summer and binding the broken pieces, they can last for at least ten years.

Many trainers will have three flights of hurdles in a straight line, with about 70 yards between them. Each individual hurdle is about six feet in length, and a whole flight is usually three hurdles, making a span of 18 feet. But if the cash stands it, you are better with four to a flight, making a wider span of 24 feet. I might be wrong about the measurements, but if you walk the course on any jump track, you will see that about six to eight hurdles make a flight, from which you can form your own conclusions.

Although most trainers put their hurdles in a straight line, I think that especially for a small trainer with limited land and cash, it is better to have your jumps in a circuit, or at least half a circuit. The ideal is to have a complete circuit of at least 1¼ miles, so that you can show the horse exactly what is expected when he runs. Not only is it a help to have the hurdles wide enough (four to a flight instead of three, and never two), but also a lot of disasters can be averted by using sensible wings.

Always use a hedge or sound fence where possible, since this eliminates one wing. To make the other wing satisfactory needs care and trouble. The wing is there only to stop the horse from running out, therefore it must be formidable. A good post, let well into the ground at the end of the flight and standing seven feet in height, is the first item, then another smaller post, equally well-installed but only four feet out of the ground, then two good long poles about 16 feet in length to be nailed approximately two feet apart on to the two stout posts.

The next important step is to make sure the angle is right. Many racecourses do not seem to pay enough attention to this. If your wing is at right angles, it is useless and dangerous. It invites a horse to duck out, and if he is prevented from doing so by his jockey, it can mean a head-on crash into the stout wing. A further 20° of angle will reduce the temptation to run out, and if it does happen, the horse will strike the solid wing a glancing blow, which is less likely to cause serious injury to the horse's chest or shoulder.

Whilst discussing wings, a word about plastic ones. Although I have not yet seen one, I have learned enough about them to discover they are fragile, as opposed to being solid. On that knowledge I would condemn them, especially on the schooling ground in the early stage. The same lesson learned by the horse who fails to clear the tree trunk and hits his shin is learned if it tries to run out through a well-made wing. "The burned child fears the fire."

As regards plastic wings being safer for both man and horse, I am also sceptical. A horse who runs out and takes on the wing will usually suffer an unpleasantly awkward fall.

The fact that he is trying to jump about five feet at an angle of 45° will cause a fall in 99 cases out of 100, and because of this oblique angle, the horse falls slap on its side and does not do the usual head-on somersault we know so well. The rider suffers because he is not thrown clear, as he usually is in a head-on fall. His leg will still be in position and the 10cwt of horseflesh falling from five feet will crash on it and break it. That is how many jockeys have broken their legs when going through the wing; it has not been, as one so often reads, due to striking a solid wing with his foot or leg. I think that if the wing was made of cardboard or even paper, the same fall would result, but I am getting too old now to feel inclined to prove my point!

However, once a horse has learned that he cannot go through a jump or a wing, I see no reason, if it is more economical, why plastic jumps and wings should not be used for more-advanced schooling. If in time we can drive on to the gallop with a tractor and trailer and erect half a dozen flights of hurdles, plus wings, in a matter of 30 minutes, it will be a move in the right direction. There are many fields in which the farmer will grant permission to canter, provided you close the gate, but naturally he will not allow permanent jumps to be installed. If one could move the jumps, it would certainly help, but I doubt if we will ever see it as such an easy operation as this.

A few further hints may be of help, and although they are obvious, one often sees disasters caused by people ignoring them.

1. Always protect the horse with boots in front, and behind as well if you have them. Many a horse's tendon has been severed by an overreach which a boot would have saved.
2. Always put up the best and most experienced man to school a novice horse, and teach your novice rider on the schoolmaster horse, who will accompany the younger one.

3. Put the novice jumper on the side where he is least likely
   to run out. If you have a wall or stout hedge on the right
   side of the hurdle, it is a fairly safe bet that with a horse
   on its left side, he can't run out.
4. Do not allow them to go too fast at the hurdle. A canter,
   increased in the final five yards, is the ideal. Flat out for
   100 yards and then a slowing-up process into the jump is
   useless.
5. Make sure the novice rider on the older horse does not
   take too much for granted. For instance, he needs to have
   his whip in his left hand if he is approaching the hurdle
   with an exposed left-hand wing. He also needs to hold his
   horse to the speed of the novice and to increase stride for
   stride over the jump; then to steady again and repeat the
   performance at the next. Because horses are to a certain
   extent copy-cats, the young horse will learn from the
   schoolmaster.

If it is possible to carry out a schooling programme of this
sort, a three-year-old selling plater who can win over seven
furlongs on the Flat and has the build for jumping is a good
thing in a three-year-old hurdle race early on in the season.
What is more, if you have really taught him how to jump,
he will climb to greater heights as a jumper than ever he could
achieve on the Flat.

18

Making Schooling Fences

One cannot make adequate steeplechase schooling fences for nothing; not only do you need cash but also the "know-how". If you do not have the knowledge for a "do-it-yourself" job, the best policy is to approach a nearby racecourse and hope their fence-builder can be persuaded to do the job for you. It will cost money, but is worth it.

When my father started training in 1905, he obtained help from Hurst Park, in this way, and had enough sense to watch every move made by the experts. From then on, his schooling ground was not unlike Hurst Park, and if anything was not quite so sharp because of its larger circuit, and therefore could be claimed to be better. That he learned how to build the fences, and made sure his men knew the drill, ensured that for the next 40 years he always had perfectly-made jumps.

It is essential to have well-made schooling fences since it is common sense that if a novice chaser is to tackle racecourse fences for the first time, he cannot be expected to do well if a broken-down jump or a few gorse bushes are all he has been shown.

The good hurdler who has run countless times without falling will not suddenly change to steeplechasing. It is a different job, requiring more effort on the horse's part, and a more deliberate effort. The hurdler can sometimes get away with it, by bending his knees at the right time, but unless he learns to get back on his hocks and jump, he will not be a success as a chaser. The only way to effect the change from hurdles to fences is to give the horse a chance to learn what is expected of him. I have known many good hurdlers who would not accept fences, and others, usually bigger and slower types, who were far better suited to them. But all needed schooling before the trainer could decide on their future.

If the new trainer starts as a jumping trainer, he may encounter the hunter-type, described by his owner as the safest jumper in the Blankshire Country. My experience was that these horses were "lethal" when it came to jumping at racing pace. They were set in their ways, used to doing it all in their own time, and became completely confused when asked to accelerate into a steeplechase fence.

The point-to-point horse is a different prospect, since he will have received the right treatment to convert a hurdler into a chaser. Small, well-made point-to-point fences are big enough to make the horse "look" and realise that it is not a hurdle, but they are not so large that they frighten him and he loses his nerve.

For years Irish horses have done remarkably well over fences in this country. In Ireland the steeplechase fences are slightly smaller than ours and this tends to build up confidence, so that their horses will take on Cheltenham or Aintree when asked to do so.

I remember Tom Walls, the actor who won the Derby with April the Fifth, had a National candidate called, I think, Crafty Alice. I still recall Press photographs of Tom's enormous schooling fence, and my father's caustic comments. The jump looked to be about 5ft. 7in. high and only about 4 yards from one frail-looking wing to the other. It was far too high and far too narrow to be any help to Crafty Alice, and it took a lot of persuasion to prevent my father from ringing up his old friend Tom Walls and telling him so!

In the same way that four hurdles in a flight are better than three or two, it is essential to make the schooling fence wide enough — 15 ft. is a minimum, and the wider the better. The height should not exceed 4ft. 3ins. but the fences do need to be stiff and to be sloped and made attractive-looking from the horse's point of view.

The way I have built a fence of this sort is as follows:—

Cut some young birch 10 to 12 feet in height from the ground and make bundles, tied closely with two bindings, Each bundle should contain 20 to 30 branches, and the reason for young birch is that you do not want thick stems in the top of the fence. Allow 60 to 80 bundles for one fence, according to your breadth. In making the timber frame, a sound back rail is important since if it breaks, your birch will fall out. I used pine trees (circumference about 14 ins.) but stout rails will do. You then need at least six stout posts for uprights, to hold the rail.

Next dig a trench the full length of the intended jump, to a depth of 2ft 6in and wide enough to take two bundles of birch one in front of the other. Now drive in your six uprights and fix the back rail to stand about 2ft. from the ground. Also at this stage it is best to put in the wing posts immediately beside the end uprights. These posts need to be 7ft. to 8ft. out of the ground and secure. It is now time to put in some birch, and the best way I found to do this was to put in six bundles at a time in the back of the trench, making sure that they are upright. Any sloping will come later. Then place six more bundles immediately in front and using a rope, tighten as much as you can and fasten to the end tall post. Fill in the trench and ram in the soil as you proceed. When the halfway mark is reached and about 36 bundles are roped tightly together, go to the other end and repeat the process, leaving the centre to last, when you pack in the final bundles. Untie the ropes and you should have an upright fence standing 10 ft. high.

The next stage is trimming, and for this all you need are a good pair of garden shears and a pruning cutter. Start behind the fence and, unless you have a good eye, place a line which will enable you to keep straight and to the required height. Cut across the fence for as far as you can comfortably reach; and to keep level, it is best to use the shears reverse side up when doing the top, kneeling down and clipping with the points facing the sky for the back. In a matter of three hours the back view of the fence should look as it will remain. Throw away or burn all the big pieces of birch trimmings, but keep all the smaller bits.

You now start on the sloping process from the front, and although this is more interesting, it is just as hard work. Start clipping at approximately the height of 2ft. 6in. and gradually slope the fence to meet your squared-off back section. You will find there are many gaps and holes, and this is where your clippings come in. Take a handful at a time, thrust them, stems first, into any gaps, and trim them to suit.

The fence should now look like the finished article, though however hard one tries for a good slope, one never seems to achieve it. This is when a facing of gorse or spruce can help. Working from the ground, start placing gorse at least two feet from the bottom of the jump and thread or push it into the birch. Trim neatly and finish off approximately 2ft. from the top of the fence. We must complete the job with a plank, board or rail, which keeps the gorse intact and gives the horse something with which to measure his jump. A board at the bottom is better than a strip of wood 18in. from the ground, and with this you can bind the gorse into position halfway up with string, which will not be seen.

We used, in the old days, to make a complete frame before we put in the birch, leaving the front part showing and placing the gorse above and below this rail. However, it meant more work and timber, and it seems modern fences have more slope by having a back to the fence as described.

As regards cost, which is where we came in on this subject a professional job might cost as much as £100 per fence, but if one is fit enough and has the knowledge, it can be done for nearer £5 a fence. Birch is often growing, self-seeded, where it is unwanted, and an observant new jump trainer could spot this and obtain permission to clear some of it. Likewise, gorse is often more of a hindrance to its owner than an asset. Timber is not really a large item and it is surprising how much suitable spare timber is lying around.

When I needed a large telegraph pole for my open ditch guard rail, I found that the post office in the middle of Chester would gladly give me one, and I bravely set off to collect it in my ancient, ex-Army, 3-ton Dodge lorry. Fortunately, in those days, people were not so fussy as they are now, and the fact that the end of my pole was making the shoppers in Chester dodge or skip did not seem to matter unduly.

A good man given all the ingredients could build a fence in two days. A new trainer, working only in the afternoons, would no doubt take a week to make the jump, adding on time for the birch to be cut and timber to be assembled for the wings.

The problem of fence-building will, I fear, become worse as skilled labour becomes scarcer. This is why we see so few good novice hurdlers coming out as five-year-olds and winning over fences first time out. Bula, an older horse, proved with Fred Winter's expert training and facilities for schooling, that a hurdler can be produced over fences first time out to show his best, but this is by no means the rule today.

Most horses have to teach themselves by trial and error on the racecourse, because their trainers cannot afford an ideal schooling ground at home. The ideal, in my opinion, should consist of three or four small fences, 3ft. in height set close together (35 yards apart), and a complete circuit of at least three full-size plain fences, an open ditch and a water jump. If this is ever possible again, we will be back to the average field for a novice steeplechase being 16 and not 6 as it often is today.

If fences are well-made in the first place, they should last for at least five years without being completely rebuilt. One can do them up each autumn by adding fresh birch and gorse, which is not a long job, and to whitewash the wings and take-off board is a simple task. After five years or more, a complete re-start is usually required, because your original birch has become rotten, and also possibly your upright posts, which hold the frame in position. The easiest way to keep the schooling ground in the right order, especially if you cannot afford £100 per fence, is to "do up" different jumps each autumn; and not to allow the whole lot to become derelict at the same time.

A water jump sounds an elaborate item to include, but it presents no trouble. A small fence of 2ft. 6in. and either a tarpaulin or corrugated iron sheets laid behind it to cover about 12ft., are all that is required. Some people use chalk in a shallow ditch and others put down boards painted white, but it really makes little difference what is used, provided the horse can see as he takes off that he has 12ft. or so to clear on the far side. Since the fence is so small, it is easier to build and will need less attention than bigger ones, which will be hit from time to time by careless jumpers.

Now you have made the jumps, you will need to find the right man to school the horses. Otherwise you are as well off to shut the horse in a loose school and let it teach itself. In that way you will save a lot of hard work and cash, but I doubt if you will make a name for yourself as a good trainer of steeplechasers.

19

To Make a Jockey

From 1975 girls are being allowed to ride on equal terms with men on the Flat. Whether girls will hold their own with men as jockeys is a moot point. Personally, I think that if the weights remain as they are today, girls will have no hope at all. Seven stones or even eight,is a very light weight for anyone, and as physical strength comes into race-riding more than most people realise, I cannot see the laws of nature being defied. Therefore, I stick my neck out and say that only about one woman in a thousand will equal a man (of the same light weight of 8st) as a Flat-race jockey.

Having upset the Women's Lib brigade with that prophecy, I will now say that a great help to Britain's labour shortage in racing the announcement has been. Whereas girls were coming into racing more for the love of it, they will now have a greater incentive than just "doing" their two or three horses.

One can presume that if girls and boys are to be treated as equals on the turf as well as under it, as Edgar Wallace would have said, apprenticeship indentures will be the same for both sexes. However, to venture another prophecy, I think this will not be the case, and that in the near future we shall see the end of apprenticeship indentures as we know them today.

The system which has worked so well for many years seems outdated. The principle whereby the trainer contracted to teach the boy to be both stableman jockey, and to feed, clothe and give him pocket money, in return for half or one-third of the boy's earnings as a jockey during apprenticeship, was a good one in far-off days. It encouraged the trainer to take on the boy in the first place with the hope, however faint it was, of making him a jockey and perhaps earning as much as £1,000 a year for his half of the boy's earnings. Today it is very different. The boy will talk to those mates leaving school at the same time and will soon learn that nobody is going in for a similar form of apprenticeship. The least, he is told, they are about to earn is £7 a week, and that is only for making cups of tea. The boy naturally weakens in his resolution to become a champion jockey and joins the queue for good wages and less graft.

The modern trainer also looks on the apprenticing business in a different way, realising that his outlay will be between £12 and £15 a week. He then considers how remote is the chance of making that boy into a good jockey, and further realises that if the miracle happens and the boy has 100 rides and 25 winners in two years time, his share of the spoils will amount to only £1,000 (approximately), if the boy has been winning the ordinary races that one would expect. Whereas 25 years ago £1,000 was a nice reward for all the work and worry put in by the trainer in order to teach the boy, today it is not enough to tempt him. So he puts an advert in the paper — "Wanted, good lad to ride work, 8 stone, must have served apprenticeship . . . " He is hoping in fact that somebody else will apprentice the boys, and when all trainers do that, I need hardly be a prophet to say that apprenticeship as we know it will cease of its own accord, if not by Jockey Club jurisdiction.

However, whether the young people you take on call themselves apprentices or not, and whether you still get your half or one-third of their earnings on the racecourse, you will still have to teach them to ride.

Stanley Wootton set an example in the best way to tackle

the job in the 1920's and 1930's, when he produced many
good jockeys, including Charlie Smirke, Staff Ingham and
Jackie Sirett to name but three from a steady supply of very
capable riders. They all seemed to bear a sort of Stanley
Wootton trade-mark, which comprised good manners,
common sense, and an inclination for hard work. In order to
achieve such a wonderful record Wootton was in the fortunate
position of being able to afford to own nearly every horse in
the yard. He would then make full use of the numerous
selling races we had in those days, putting up a boy who had
shown promise on one of his useful old platers when it had a
definite winning chance. If the boy took full advantage of
this opportunity, he would be put up again in similar
circumstances, and with the confidence gained from a couple
of early wins, he usually went on from strength to strength.
Often boys who can ride quite well become disheartened by
having what few rides are available on horses which have no
chance whatsoever. In this way they lose the hope and
confidence they would have gained with Wootton's treatment.

A further advantage for the boys in Wootton's yard was
that as nearly everyone in the stable was a jockey, and often
a very good one, the beginner always had someone to copy
when riding work; and there is no better way of improving
one's ability at any game or sport than by continually
competing with experts.

I believe the discipline was strict, and any boy who did not
ride to orders would receive one of Stanley Wootton's pep-
talks on the lines: "My boy, I think it will be better for you
not to ride out for a week and to give yourself time for
reflection. I suggest that you dig my garden instead."
I remember watching a race in which one of his junior
apprentices had ridden a wild but apparently effective finish.
I asked Stanley, "What will that one make?" The answer
came in his well-known pedantic tone: "A dashing young

cavalryman no doubt, but, alas, never a jockey." He was right too.

I have quoted Wootton as the best example of a trainer who set out to make jockeys, because he seemed the only one, apart from Major Sneyd, who did not give up the struggle to concentrate on training winners instead. So many trainers who have specialised at it and have been highly successful, have found out that if you want to keep good owners and train high-class horses, the use of unskilled apprentices soon puts an end to your ambition.

It is not because some trainers cannot teach their boys to ride that they never produce a good apprentice jockey; many of them could do a Stanley Wootton process all over again in the same circumstances. But when they have a stable full of horses at an average value of £10,000 a piece, how are they to do it? The trainer who is just starting does, however, have a better chance than the men at the top of the tree. It is unlikely the beginner's recent purchases will be quite so costly, and he may have at least one owner who won't object to giving a boy or girl a chance to practise.

The first stage of teaching a boy or girl, aged 16 and who has never ridden a horse, is not so formidable as it sounds, provided you have a suitable horse and some form of enclosure in which to do the job. If you have neither, it is a matter of sending the learners out on their feet to ride back as your horses return from morning exercise. However, this is slower than putting the pupil on a quiet horse in a riding school and teaching basic horsemanship.

This is what Johnny Gilbert is now doing at Stone-leigh, and there is no doubt that in an establishment of that sort, with all the aids, the first principles can be taught better and quicker than at home. It is when the pupil has learned enough to have confidence, yet nothing like enough to be considered an adequate horseman by anybody apart from himself, that the trouble starts.

To be a good jockey you must first be a horseman, which means learning to ride in the conventional way. Once this object is achieved, you can adopt any style you like. If ultra-short is the rage, you ride ultra-short; if jockeys decide to ride full length of their leg, as their ancestors did, you can also oblige. The now-confident pupil does not listen to this advice, and after seeing Flat-race jockeys on T.V. and his own companions riding out, he decides he will never be a jockey unless he pulls up his leathers. What is worse, he thinks the shorter he rides the better jockey he will be. The result is that having arrived in a position on the horse' back of which any contortionist would be jealous, he is entirely without grip, balance or anything else which he was starting to acquire. Now is the time to take a firm line with the pupil, and whether it is a boy or girl tell them that if they expect any rides or help from you in the future, they must ride exactly as they are told. Apprentices who continually disobey you about the length of their leathers will still disobey you in the unlikely event of their becoming jockeys, and they are not worth your sacrifices.

If you are to produce your apprentice on a horse with a winning chance, it is surprising how many sacrifices do take place. Here are three instances:

1. If it is your own horse which looks to have a reasonable chance in a selling handicap with 8st, and you know that with the best jockey in the saddle it would be a good betting prospect and would pay for a year's keep by winning.

2. When you have told several white lies to your most faithful owner about how one more race will do no harm, and how much better the horse goes for this particular apprentice.

3. When your owner particularly wants to run in a jockeys'

race at Kempton, but you have promised the boy a ride on the same day in the apprentice race at Warwick. This entails more white lies to convince the owner how Warwick will be more suitable.

All these are sacrifices, especially if, as is usually the case, the poor apprentice loses a race which he should have won, through no fault other than lack of practice.

Although I have tried to explain that today it is almost impossible to produce good jockeys and still keep owners and train the maximum of winners, I hope that when the Levy Board and the Joint Racing Authorities find a bit of spare cash, they will give thought to two simple ideas. Neither should come as a shock to them, as I have tried in my own way to put them over for the last ten years.

(a) Every trainer with three or more apprentices should be allowed the free keep and racing expenses for one horse to be used solely to teach apprentices.

(b) A jockeys' training school should be established, consisting of 20 racehorses in training and to race throughout the year, paid for by the Levy Board. The trainer and his head man would be the instructors; the labour would comprise ten apprentices on eight-week courses throughout the year. Private races would be run, entirely for the inmates of the school, at the nearest racecourse and involving the horses at the school and anyone who wished to give their horses a gallop.

It possibly seems a wild idea, but it does happen in other countries, and there is only one place to make jockeys, and that is in their natural surroundings, a racing stable. One can lecture them on subjects which will further their racing education; one can teach them the principles of basic horse-manship. But one will never make them jockeys without constant practice on the gallops and the racecourse. Today there hardly seems to be a trainer in the country with the time, money or inclination to concentrate on making a jockey. Yet because of the vast increase in the horse population, jockeys were never more needed.

20

Dealings with the Bank

In my old home at Weyhill there were many paintings and photographs of famous horses, one of which I very much regret has gone astray.

It was a caricature, drawn in 1878 and depicting a bankruptcy court hearing held in rather unusual circumstances. The judge in his wig and robe, was standing in what appeared to be the rostrum of a racecourse sale ring. The jockey, my great uncle Garrett Moore, and his horse Liberator, were in the unsaddling enclosure marked "Dock", and the judge was leaning down to hear Garry's whisper, which was to tell him to get his cash on Liberator for the National, which he duly won in March 1879, putting Garrett Moore, who rode him and owned him back in business.

This sketch was entitled "The Liberator", and not only was it clever but it also showed how in racing you can be on the floor one minute and back in the money two months later.

However, this scene was set in Southern Ireland nearly 100 years ago, which no doubt explains why Garrett Moore was allowed a bit of time! I am afraid today your bank manager, when approached with a tale of how much you intend to win in the near future, will take a line from Omar Khayyam, and tell himself, "Ah, take the cash in hand and waive the rest; oh, the brave music of a distant drum!"

Unless a racehorse trainer owns his property or farms as a

side line, he is in a very bad position regarding an overdraft. A farmer, even if he rents his farm as you do your stable, will have valuable stock, growing crops and machinery as security towards an overdraft on his *business*, whereas all the trainer can hope for is a *personal* overdraft based on such as his life policy. In one of my many financial crises as a trainer I offered the bank my horsebox, valued at £1,200, as security, but the bank regretted they could not accept my offer, as the box would not fit into their vaults!

It is a pity that the large turnover involved does not carry more weight with banks when they consider an overdraft. If for your stable of ten horses you are charging £25 per horse per week, you have a yearly turnover of £13,000. However, even if this is doubled or trebled, according to the number of fully paid-for horses you have in the yard, the manager will be far more interested in seeing the evidence of your last season's training account figures. These, I am sorry to say, will on three occasions out of five show a loss, unless you are in the top 20 trainers' bracket. Therefore you will suffer a long, friendly, but entirely frustrating lecture from the manager, on these lines: "You must realise that although we want to help you, and it is our job to lend money to help people build up their business, we are not allowed to grant overdrafts unless there are signs that a repayment will be made."

You will find this load of codswallop dished up in a slightly altered form by bank managers all over the country. There is not much you can do about it, unless you take the drastic action of the trainer who, finding himself in possession of six yearlings at the Dublin Sales but with no money in the bank, sent a wire to his manager saying, "Have bought you six nice yearlings".

Racing being the up-and-down specialised occupation which it is, one cannot expect the average bank manager to understand what goes on. He can do his homework on the farming industry, or on builders and contractors, and he knows where he is amongst shopkeepers and professional men like lawyers, doctors and dentists. Racehorse trainers, however, are not fee-earning folk, (unless they are private ones earning a fixed salary), whereas their employees are, and a jockey has a set fee for each ride. The public trainer therefore has no set wage coming in each week, apart from the cash from his owners, which goes out as fast as it comes in.

All my life, so far, I have been in a position where an overdraft of some sort was essential, and I feel entitled to drop a few hints to the trainer about to start up in business. Firstly, you should make the most of the fact that you are just starting. You go to your bank and tell the manager how you are "about to set the Thames on fire" during the next few years, and how necessary it is to have his help in order to buy tack, make alterations, and buy a horse box, etc.

Having so far avoided the manager's pep-talk, go for the biggest overdraft you can get on your life policy, or whatever it is which you are handing over. It is no good saying you can scrape by on, say, a £1,000 overdraft, when you will be trying to double or treble it in three years time. That is where I went wrong, finding that although I had the security to stand a larger overdraft, the manager then gave me the pep-talk. He rummages slowly and carefully through your last two seasons' accounts, as drawn up by the accountant who has charged you about £50 for the job, then looks over his spectacles and says: "I see by your last two seasons' training figures that your business is showing a slight loss. Now, although our bank's policy is to help . . . "

You leave the bank with your £1,000 overdraft, but no increases, and unpleasant phrases like "You are really insolvent, you know"; "Can't you do another job?" etc.

ringing in your ears. It is then you realise what a mug you were not to try harder for a bigger overdraft in the first place. Once that miserly manager has seen the figures for your two years' hard work, you have not a dog's chance — unless by some happy freak your account shows a healthy profit, in which case, as I used to try to drum into obstinate managers, you won't need an overdraft.

There are other points which I have never understood regarding banks refusing overdrafts. Why, I wonder, do they quibble about a £1,000 loan to a person they know is 100 per cent honest, but dish out £20,000 without a qualm to some "con-man" with whom they have had no previous dealings? I suppose it is greed more than anything else. Whereas little overdrafts are more of an embarrassment than anything else, a big one is a nice income for the bank. But I for one shed no tears when the "con-man" does them down.

To return to the depressing position where the trainer finds himself with his overdraft stretched to the last new penny, about £2,000 worth of bills in what I used to call the L.B.W. basket (let the beggars wait) and a full season's racing about to begin. If the bank won't play, you must try elsewhere, and this is often when your owners, if they are the right sort, will come to the rescue. With training fees as high as they are, and likely to become far higher, a £1,000 advance towards a horse's keep can get you out of a jam, and in many cases is not inconveniencing the owner. Likewise, many a wealthy man has lent money to his trainer and furthermore has not asked for the bank's percentage on the loan.

The trouble in these circumstances is that if like I do you consider it is the bank's job to lend money, provided security is offered them, you will not feel inclined to approach your friends or owners, especially at an early stage of your career.

Over the years I have filed all correspondence with the

bank and it has now moved out of the files into a tea-chest, which soon I hope to fill before I burn it all.

There are so many identical letters that I feel that all banks must have the same formula. The letters start: "Dear .... I am sorry but I must point out to you that your account now stands at £1,005.7p. Whereas, as you are aware, our agreed figure is for an overdraft of £1,000 net. I must therefore ask you not to issue any further cheques . . ." The letters all finish with kind inquiries after one's health and the family's, and almost a "Love Jack" ending, but at the time they are a a worry. It is all right saying "don't issue any further cheques", but in the same post you will possibly have two final demands for payment within seven days, and where do you go from there? Either you go to the money-lenders, a friend or an owner — all because that wretched man at the bank would not give you the overdraft to which you think you are entitled.

To end this depressing chapter on a lighter vein, I must admit I have had plenty of fun from my love-hate relationship with various bank managers. I have always received courtesy; and if an application has been turned down, it has been done politely. My dealings with hire-purchase firms, however, have been a very different story.

In 18 years as a trainer I had a number of horseboxes. Unfortunately, three ended up as write-offs after accidents, but as far as I remember the insurance paid up. The last one I owned cost £2,500 when bought, and I still owed £600 to the hire-purchase firm when I decided to quit training and therefore came to sell the horse-box.

I failed to pay two of the monthly instalments, mainly because as I was selling the box, I thought, in my unenlightened way, that I would settle up when it was sold. However, while taking an afternoon nap with a bad go of 'flu, I had a most abusive call from the hire-purchase people, to whom

I had paid some £5,000 over the years. I was accused of being every sort of a crook; I had not paid for two months, I had no right to sell the horse box without their consent etc. It was their's, they said. Feeling like death and not appreciating the tone of the man at the other end, I said, "Right, if you feel like that, you can have the box. I owe you £600 and the box will make over £1,000 in the sale. If you know how to sell it, it's all yours." The man at the other end was in a state. He was accustomed to bullying defaulting clients, but to have a horsebox thrown at him, even with the chance of a handsome profit, put him well out of his depth. I was told I could not sell the box because the firm owned, but they weakened when I told them that after all they only owned the back wheels, if I had so far paid £1,900 towards the original cost. The result was that I did sell, for around £1,000, and paid the hire-purchase firm their £600, but if they had had the sense to accept my rash offer, they would have made a further £400.

In view of this experience I regard banks as the lesser of two evils and would advise dealing with them in preference to a hire-purchase company. You should keep hire-purchase folk to the level of the television, deep freeze and washing machine; but don't let them get their teeth into anything bigger.

21

To Have a Side Line

As things are today it is long odds against a new trainer, with 10 to 15 horses, earning £10,000 for his owners and thus £1,000 for himself. If he wins 10 races, he can say he has done a good job. But will those races average £1,000 apiece? If you are lucky and you have won the £10,000, is £1,000 enough to live on? And how about the lean years, when you can hardly win a race of any sort?

There seems a good case nowadays for a young trainer with plenty of energy to have a side line as insurance against becoming bankrupt.

In the past Stewards of the Jockey Club apparently took a dim view of a trainer doing other jobs, no doubt because he might neglect his own work, which came under their jurisdiction. However, if the trainer was declared bankrupt, they swiftly removed his licence — and that was "rough justice".

Times have changed and as far as I know side lines such as farming, stud management, working for a bloodstock agency, owning a share in an auctioneers' business etc. are all permissable. Perhaps taking up the pen and writing an anti-Jockey Club Column in a daily paper would be sticking your head into the noose a little too far!

Managing a farm or stud, provided you hold the necessary qualifications and have time to do it, would ensure a salary to keep your head above water in a bad training year. But such jobs are unlikely to come up on your doorstep, and it is no

good taking on either unless you are on the spot. To own
and run either enterprise will need a lot of capital, and if you
have that, you won't need a side line. However, to look at it
in reverse, if you are already a farmer and decide to become
a trainer, you would be very stupid to relinquish the farm,
since it is a good combination and has been proved so for
many years.

To buy horses for a bloodstock agency is a job for which
most trainers are well placed. They should be good judges of
a horse; they attend the races nearly every day and see the
horses; and they know their fellow trainers (who will become
clients). A bloodstock agency would be wise to employ a
trainer in preference to anyone else. However, that is the
agencies' privilege, and no doubt there are good reasons for
not employing trainers. Some might be inclined to "hunt
with the hare and run with the hounds", which may influence
agencies towards a less biased man.

There must be many other side lines to help the trainer's
lot, but farming is the best.

My father owned 600 acres of farmland and had the
knowledge, with the help of his close friend and assistant,
Herbert Arnold, to run it both as a help to train his horses
and as a commercial business. In the course of nearly 50
years, every sort of farming took place; sheep, cows, beef and
corn all had their turn, and pigs and poultry were a permanent fixture. I cannot say that over the years the farm showed
a vast profit, because this was not the case. During the late
1920's and throughout the 1930's no farming paid, but as it
was run in conjunction with a racing stable, it did help.

To be able to grow a strip of lucerne or clover, and cut it
fresh in the early summer months, is a wonderful day-to-day
help to horses. To grow a good clover and rye grass mixture
or sanfoin was another asset. Oats, if good enough, would at
least do for half a year's supply, and if they were not up to

standard, which was so often the case, we could swap them for the best from Scotland at a small loss. Wheat straw when threshed out of a stack was so much cleaner and better than the stuff we buy in fusty bales today, and it was all there on the farm.

Nowadays one cannot hope to be so self-supporting, even if one could afford to run a farm of that sort; but nevertheless it is still a good side line, even if only done in a small way. Fresh-cut clover, manure to put back on the land, a patch of carrots, a strip of plough to use when the ground is hard: all help to keep the horses happy and yourself solvent.

The trouble you will encounter today is labour, a problem that faces more than racehorse trainers and farmers. In the days of which I have been writing, the agricultural worker and stableman earnt the same. If it was a busy time on the farm, at say haymaking or harvest, the trainer could divert a few of his stronger lads to help out; likewise, his farm staff would cut the "green-meat" for the horses and leave it in the yard. They could also leave the trailer in the yard to be filled with muck from the boxes and tow it to the muck-heap next day, saving the lads a long walk with a heavy load.

I am not sure that in these days of cut and thrust tactics, the attitude of "farmworkers and stablehands should be friends" will work so amicably. Everyone is so busy saying "that's not my job" that nobody gets anything done. Your farm staff will no doubt have to be kept entirely separate and be paid a different (probably much lower) wage, which is a pity, because after many years of working with and employing both, I always found complete harmony.

22

The Trainer's Future

So far I have not drawn the pretty picture of a happy life, with a secure future, for the would-be trainer, but then I never set out to do that in the first place. What is even more depressing is to look at it with the next ten years in mind.

A recent list of winning trainers published in the *Sporting Life* shows that of 239 Flat-race trainers quoted, 43 earned £20,000 or more for their owners, and 25 earned £10,000 or more. This means that 68 trainers may have got enough 10 per cent from the winnings on which to live. But how about the 171 trainers who have not earned £1,000 a year for themselves? Bear in mind also that the *Sporting Life*, being a tactful publication, only includes winning trainers. Therefore, we must accept that many more, perhaps even 50, have not won a race at all.

It is food for thought that a trainer's life depends on his 10 per cent from his owners winnings. You can have a good year and win 20 races with your 30 horses, but I doubt very much if you will earn over £1,000 for your endeavour.

Looking through the 1973 Flat racing figures, we see many people in the position in which the new trainer will find himself if he has a good year. To quote three trainers who I know well, and who are as good at the job if not better than any newcomer can hope to be:

Trainer No. 1 has had a very good year, following a very bad one, when the virus moved in. His total of 23 winners adds up to £14,826; his string would not exceed 30.

Trainer No. 2 is listed as having 35 horses in training and has won 22 races, value £14,853.

Trainer No. 3 is a Newmarket man with 46 horses, and has won 22 races, value £14,827, which no doubt is an average year for him.

These figures show the same sad story. One cannot expect to win more than one race for every two horses in the yard; and when one does achieve far better than this, one still collects under £1,500 on which to live. The reasons are fairly obvious, since stake money for ordinary races, which are the ones you will hope to win, remains very low indeed. An early two-year-old race is by no means a push-over, but you will often only get 10 per cent of a £307 stake. There are, of course, plenty of sponsored races worth the earth, but you will find that you do not have the horses to enter for them.

However, if you are lucky, your statistics could read as one trainer's do — 2 winners, stake money earned £35,477. That man has done a short cut, but this can only happen by having a good horse in the yard, and fate often decrees that this never happens.

If a trainer's future is to be secure, the level of stake money must be raised, and no Flat race should be worth less than £1,500 to the winner. At present, as the three examples show, the average is approximately £500, which in time will force the small trainer to pack in his job. When this happens, the already overcrowded, successful yards will take in more and more horses. This, unfortunately, has already become the trend.

There are more stables with over 80 horses than ever in this country. We then have to ask ourselves, "Can any person today, with the sort of labour available, train over 80 horses really well?" Trainers — being trainers — say "yes they can", if they have 80 horses, and "no they can't," if they have 30 horses themselves.

Looking at it from a neutral angle, it would seem that a large stable (and some have well over 100 horses) will win large stake money, as one would expect with increased opportunity, but as regards ration of races won per horse in the yard they do not come out of it very well. Only seven trainers won more than 50 races in the 1973 season, and they were all in the 80 to 100 horse yards. So it seems that for training winners the small stables of 30 horses who produce 20 winners are doing the better job.

Another factor to consider is the number of horses involved who do "bring home the bacon". For instance, the leading trainer amassed a total of £132,984 with only 21 horses involved; so there must have been at least 50 horses in his yard who had a blank year. This is a point that owners should consider before they flock to an already over-stocked yard.

The slogan "If you can't beat them, join them" is the best advice for the future small trainer. Even if lack of capital has forced you to start in a small way, you must always think in a big way, and hope for the day when you have 60 horses under your care. In this way the law of averages will ensure that your 10 per cent of earnings on stake money won does produce enough to keep the wolf from the door.

To look at the problem with the future of British racing at heart, it seems entirely wrong that we should reach a state where trainers, provided they have enough private means, can virtually buy success, whereas men with more knowledge, and who have started at the foot of the ladder, cannot hope to survive. If this trend continues, and at the same time labour is not properly trained, I see trouble ahead in a big way. It is because of the thorough background and working knowledge possessed by former generations of trainers that our race-horses have reached their high standard in the racing world today. Once this expertise is lost, the standard must surely drop, and then other countries which have learned our methods will take the lead.

Understandably, readers might think that as I gave up training because I could not afford to continue, I wear a chip on my shoulder and I am inclined to paint too black a picture of the trainer's cares. I can assure them this is not the case, and if I ever come into a bit of cash, I will renew the challenge. It is a good life and an interesting one. One could say there is never a dull moment, which is a lot more than can be said about most jobs. It is the money concern which will hold me in check until I see a move in the right direction by the authorities.

We obviously have too many horses in training for the existing racing executive to deal with. This means (to put it bluntly and unkindly) a sigh of relief goes up when a trainer or owner quits the Turf. But how do we alter the situation?

Studs keep producing horses for sale; new owners are prepared to spend an average of £5,000 for a yearling, and general interest in racing, possibly due to T.V., increases all the time. It seems unlikely, therefore, that the next decade will see fewer horses in training, But it does seem that fewer trainers and lads will be around to look after them. This in turn will lead to the build-up of very large stables, as has happened in the past in France, Ireland and the U.S.A.

My solution is to increase the administration to cater for more horses, and to take a great deal more money from the betting industry.

When we seemed to step out of line was on the day we started to put the cart before the horse, when it was assumed that as the punter was indirectly subsidising the owner, the owner held some sort of debt to the punter. This seems to me to be wrong, unless punters own all the horses. You might just as well say that we should all be allowed in free to the local theatre, because indirectly we are ploughing back cash via the rates. We must have a spectacle, and whether we watch it or bet on it as well, is our own choice; but we cannot have it at all unless somebody pays to produce the show. The person who pays in the case of racing is the owner, and he does not pay "chicken-feed" either.

If in the future the owner is considered first, I see a good prospect for everybody; but if not, it will mean an entirely different outlook. We could finish with nothing but syndicated stables, with four owners running them and a private trainer installed. If this comes about and the aspiring trainer can get in on it, a lot of the trainer's cares will be dispersed with and it will also lead to a higher standard of training. However, I think that you will find much of the fun goes too.

It is the constant struggle which makes training such an interesting job. The fights with the bank manager, lack of staff, trouble with the Stewards, non-paying owners, bad horses and virus infections: they all add up to a very happy life "if you don't weaken".

Since I first sat down to write this book the Trainers lot has changed more than at any time in our racing history.

Lads' wages continually increase. Fodder goes up by leaps and bounds. Mr. Tom Blackwell's Report suggests a minimum training charge, and for an alteration to the apprentice indenture system. On the brighter side there is to be a slight increase in the overall stake money.

In view of these changes, and no doubt countless more to come, I have not rewritten in order to catch up. If I did so, I fear that I might discourage the new young trainer even further and that as you know is not my intention. "I never promised you a rose garden!"

J.H. Hartigan
1975

Readers of this book who wish to be informed about new and forthcoming publications on horses, horsemanship, racing and breeding are invited to send their names and addresses to:

J.A. Allen & Co. Ltd.,
1 Lower Grosvenor Place,
Buckingham Palace Road,
London, SW1W 0EL